Praise for

T0276743

"A thoroughly researched primer and [...] on a decade of community-based [...] demand for abolition of the prison industrial complex, [...] teous call to reclaim sovereignty over the shared places we call home. It shows us how the struggle for housing as a human right is more than that: it's a class struggle for land and power, so life can thrive. READ THIS BOOK."
            —**susan rosenberg**, prison and human rights activist

"The American dream of homeownership has turned into a nightmare of landlord and bank profits, unpayable mortgages, sky high rents, evictions, and unnecessary suffering. At once an insightful manifesto for a new housing paradigm that can provide shelter for every human being and a shrewd tactical guide, *Abolish Rent* can help us build a tenant-powered movement capable of winning the radical change we need. This urgent book is a rousing wake up call that can help snap us out of our collective slumber and into collective action."
            —**Astra Taylor**, cofounder of the Debt Collective
            and author of *The Age of Insecurity*

"A spectre is haunting landlords—the spectre of land seizures & rent strikes. *Abolish Rent* provides clear analysis and vivid stories of Los Angeles grassroots tenants, whose efforts offer a path towards abolishing commodification of land and housing. The authors situate tenant struggles as essential in today's worldwide movement to secure dignity, or as Isabel Garcia of Boyle Heights says in this book: 'We fight because we have to continue living.'"
            —**Ruth Wilson Gilmore**, author of *Abolition Geography*, and
            Craig Gilmore, cofounder of the California Prison Moratorium Project

"This essential book provides a concise history of racist, colonial housing policy and its central role in racial capitalism; an accessible analysis of the injustice and illegitimacy of rent; inspiring accounts of effective tenant resistance; and a crystal clear call for collective action that we can all take up right now. While rents skyrocket, police budgets bloat, wealth consolidates, and global temperatures rise, we need this book. *Abolish Rent* shows why we don't need more empty declarations of our rights, more policy reforms that keep things the same, or more efforts to appeal to the moral conscience of politicians owned by the rich, we need to abolish landlords and take over where we live."
            —**Dean Spade**, author of *Mutual Aid*

"A riveting polemic and a convincing argument for why our housing system must be radically transformed. Their on-the-ground reporting is sure to persuade anyone angry at how much rent they pay that we all must organize for a better future. It goes deep into the history and theory of housing and provides tangible solutions to our housing crisis, ones that we can all take part in today."

—**P.E. Moskowitz**, author of *How to Kill a City*

"Inspiring and powerful, *Abolish Rent* is a passionate handbook of community organizing rendered through moving—even thrilling—case studies of tenants reclaiming their buildings and public space. The utopian vision of abolishing rent is potentially within our grasp."

—**Lizzie Borden**, director of *Born in Flames*

"An essential primer on rent and the collective struggle required to liberate ourselves from its grasp on our lives. Rosenthal and Vilchis give us precise language for what we're up against and equip us with deeply human stories that demonstrate how tenants might change our housing system and the world—if we take our own power seriously."

—**Tara Raghuveer**, founding director, KC Tenants

"Across America today, the social crisis is in large measure a housing crisis, and the housing crisis is in large measure a crisis of rent. This book is both an angry account of how the rental crisis came to be, and a loving paean to those at the sharp end who are coming together to take collective action and fight back. Don't miss it."

—**Brett Christophers**, author of *Our Lives in Their Portfolios*

"*Abolish Rent* is a manifesto—but it's more than that. It's an archive of the lessons learned in struggle and the deepened analysis that comes as a movement grows. The LA Tenants Union has mapped the arduous path out of the housing crisis."

—**Gabriel Winant**, author of *The Next Shift*

"This is a transformative book, one that radically shifts our attention from the seeming 'housing crisis' to the crisis that is racial capitalism and its relations of extraction and domination. It is also a hopeful book, one that centers tenants as the collectivized subjects of a space-making/world-making history."

—**Ananya Roy**, professor and director, UCLA Luskin Institute on Inequality and Democracy

"*Abolish Rent* makes the case against our system of real estate domination and for a world where tenants no longer dread the first of each month. Shifting our understanding of the crisis from one centering landlords and the state to one centering tenants, Rosenthal and Vilchis demonstrate the true toll of our extractive capitalist order and point us to the already-existing seeds of a better future—a future of liberation, solidarity, and convivencia."

—**Samuel Stein**, author of *Capital City*

ABOLISH RENT

How Tenants Can
Solve the Housing Crisis

Tracy Rosenthal and Leonardo Vilchis

Haymarket Books
Chicago, Illinois

Published in 2024 by
Haymarket Books
P.O. Box 180165
Chicago, IL 60618
www.haymarketbooks.org

ISBN: 9798888902523

Distributed to the trade in the US through Consortium Book Sales
and Distribution (www.cbsd.com) and internationally through
Ingram Publisher Services International (www.ingramcontent.com).

This book was published with the generous support of Lannan Foundation, Wallace Action Fund, and Marguerite Casey Foundation.

Special discounts are available for bulk purchases by organizations
and institutions. Please email info@haymarketbooks.org for more
information.

Cover design by David Gee.

Library of Congress Cataloging-in-Publication data is available.

Entered into digital printing September, 2024.

For Gustavo Otzoy, 1966–2023

CONTENTS

INTRODUCTION

THE TWO AUTHORS of this book spent July 4th delighting in the collective disobedience of hundreds of thousands of people across Los Angeles. On Leonardo's roof, while Tracy cheered at each blast, we watched as each gathering of friends and family knit their own fireworks into the broad sheet of LA sky. Together these explosions coalesced into hours of light and sound, which dogs hate and children love. From our perch in Boyle Heights, we toasted not to patriotism, but to possibility: it is already possible to defy the law, upend the social order, and participate in mass, collective action. Maybe this is what it would take to ensure that everyone in our city had a home.

Los Angeles often shows us the future of the whole country. As the United States incorporated LA's territory, annexing Mexico and ethnically cleansing the Tongva people—for whom the land was home for seven thousand years—the city innovated legal settlement and subjugation. More than half a century before land values became a central business of urban centers everywhere, LA's boosters were divvying downtown parcels to flip, inspiring a literary and film genre—noir—to describe real estate's political influence.[1] Already by the 1950s, Los Angeles imprisoned more people than any other city in the US, which itself imprisoned more people than any country in the world, as it still does today.[2]

Now Los Angeles shows us the future of housing inequality should we allow our capitalist housing system to continue unabated. Two years ago, our city boasted the world's most expensive home—a $340 million mansion, complete with five pools, forty-two bathrooms, and a moat—while five unhoused tenants died on our streets each day. In 1980, LA earned the title of "homeless capital of America." We still claim the largest number of unsheltered people.[3] But perhaps Los Angeles will play the part of the future for housing revolution, for beating back exploitation and domination, for undoing the rent relation itself.

THE TWO OF us might look like an odd pair, a middle-aged immigrant and a thirty-something LGBT. But there is a long history of Mexicans and Jews organizing together in California. More than that, we reflect two sides of a growing constituency: tenants in the United States.

Disproportionately shut out of homeownership or included only under predatory terms, people of color and immigrants have long found themselves exploited and oppressed within the US property regime—shunted into the subordinate status of tenants, segregated, and subject to price gouging. But that status has expanded. Intergenerational wealth transfers, rather than income, have become the determining factor of access to owning a home. Millennials can count themselves the first generation whose relationship to housing has been shaped by this new American order. So it may not be surprising that in the struggle for tenant power, we'd find each other.

We met in 2012 in a warehouse-turned-community gallery in Cypress Park. The space was both a symptom of and a response to a process we discussed that day, often euphemized as "neighborhood change," but better known as gentrification. Alongside a small, multi-racial and -generational group, we helped form School of Echoes. Our collective spent a few years listening: to STAY in Echo Park, where a gang injunction meant youth of color could be jailed just for sitting together outside; to residents of Frogtown, where a new public park arrived after half of all neighborhood properties had changed hands in three years; to Needle Exchange in Hollywood, where harm reduction operations had to keep up with stepped-up encampment sweeps; to Union de Vecinos, a Boyle Heights union of neighbors Leo had cofounded in 1996 to fight the demolition of more than nine hundred public apartments. We heard city governments announce expanded tax bases instead of services, nonprofits negotiate the terms of communities' defeat, lawyers offer individualistic advice, and tenants who thought there was nothing they could do.

Yet we knew our capitalist housing system, to use Ursula K. Le Guin's phrase, is a "human power"—produced by people, not by God or by nature. Any human power, she wrote, "can be changed by human beings." High rents, displacement, and homelessness are not inevitable. Rent as a social, political, and economic relationship is not inevitable. Our capitalist housing system can—and must—be changed. But the solidarity among its beneficiaries—landlords, developers, elected officials, the police—means we need to build equal solidarity for ourselves. In other words, we knew we couldn't fight against rent alone.

School of Echoes convened the first meeting of the LA Tenants Union (LATU) in 2015, with a single gathering in Hollywood. We invited tenants from across the city to reflect on the common features of their housing conditions and what they thought it was in their reach to control. We have since grown to over three thousand households of dues-paying members and twelve local chapters that trace the city's sprawl with our own. We have organized more than a hundred tenants associations, which have won our members needed repairs, rent rollbacks, and a measure of dignity. LATU is a member-funded union. Our meetings are monolingual in Spanish or bilingual in Spanish and English, and at times interpreted in Korean and Cantonese. As we break down the shame of living in deteriorating housing we can barely afford, we build trust across racial, ethnic, linguistic, even class differences. As we mourn for those banished from our communities, we fight like hell with those who remain. In our one-party city in our one-party state, we organize tenants as political subjects whose task it is to beat back the power of real estate and change the world.

THIS IS THE first book-length engagement with a resurgent tenant movement. Slum conditions, rent gouging, and the despotic power of private landlords over tenants' access to shelter are not new conditions. But our moment gives tenant organizing new urgency. For the first time in US history in 2021, the appreciation of the median home outstripped the median salary: just owning a home made more money than work.[4] The rent is too, too damn high. Unhoused tenants face rising criminalization, as more are flung into the streets. Our homes have become the catchall for all the crises of our times: poverty, precarity, care work, crime. In 2020, a global pandemic severed millions of tenants from their incomes nearly overnight. For millions, paying rent went from onerous to impossible. Our representatives at every level of government, tasked with stopping a flood of evictions, were content with turning down the faucet. Tenants looked to each other.

Thousands of tenants across the country have joined a nascent effort to turn our individualized vulnerability into shared power. Our tactics—tenants associations, rent strikes, occupations— rhyme with the heyday of tenant militancy. In the Bay Area, DC, Kansas City, Louisville, Houston, New York, and more cities throughout the country, tenants are organizing not just to win better living conditions, but to overturn the power relations that shape those conditions altogether. At the onset of the pandemic, the LA Tenants Union more than tripled in size, engaging thousands of tenants who couldn't pay rent, our local force resonating with the international demand that all rent payments accrued during the pandemic be canceled. The inspiration for this book came from both those moments when we thought reality had endorsed another way of living together, and when the brutality we call normal reasserted itself as the rule.

The housing question is, at its center, a question about inequality: who gets to be housed and who doesn't, who profits from housing and who falls into poverty paying or failing to pay the rent. It is also a question about power: who gets to decide how we organize our cities and how we organize our lives. It is a matter of life and death. This book looks at the housing question not from the perspective of governments (who see it as a problem to be managed) nor of developers and landlords (who see it as an opportunity for predation) but of tenants, whose lives are constrained and destroyed, but also enabled and enriched, by where we live.

This book is both polemic and guide. It begins from the assumption that everyone deserves a safe and stable home, or the right to use public space as they wish, simply by virtue of being alive. This is what we mean when we say housing is a human right, no different than the right to breathe the air on this earth: you are born with this

right; you should not have to earn it; you should not have to work for
it. For us, "Housing is a human right" is not a slogan meant to urge
us to tinker at the margins of a broken system. It is not an ideal for
which we should calmly strive. Every second we live when housing
is not respected as a human right is a violation. We remain stuck in
this degraded world by means of exploitation and domination, by an
economic system that enriches landlords by extracting wealth from
tenants, by a political system that enshrines the right to private gains
over public good, the right to property over the right to life.

"Housing is a human right" has become a cliché because we
continue to let the people who violate our rights off the hook. There
are violators of our rights: the hoarders of space and wealth, against
whom we defend our communities, and from whom we are owed
the fruits of our common labor, the value of our homes and neighborhoods. The failure to provide a basic human need in the richest country in the history of the world is not an aberration of the
capitalist housing system, but that system working as designed; the
production of wealth for a few and misery for the many is its engine
and its purpose.

Another world will not simply be handed over. To overthrow
the exploitation and domination of the present order will take a liberatory struggle. It is a struggle to forge new democratic structures
for managing and distributing resources according to our needs. It
is a struggle against those whose wealth and power is made on the
backs of our demise. Those who are now the most vulnerable to the
violence and injustice of our current system have the most to gain
by its destruction and the creation of another way of life. We want a
world without landlords and a world without rent. We want everything for everyone.

THIS BOOK IS grounded in the concrete struggles of tenants to gain control over our housing, our cities, and our lives—that really existing movement to abolish the present state of things. First, we ground the necessity of this transformation. Chapter 1 is a polemic against rent: a power relation between landlords and tenants, an axis of class exploitation and domination, a tribute that we pay at the peril of our need and at the barrel of a gun. Chapter 2 is an abridged history of the long "war on tenants," the love affair between real estate and the state.

We then describe what tenants are already doing to bring ourselves closer to the world we deserve. In our individual buildings, we can contest the despotic control landlords have over our access to a home. Chapter 3 describes a successful yearlong rent strike in Boyle Heights as an example and model of what tenant organizing makes possible. In our citywide unions, we can build a countervailing force to the real estate regime. Chapter 4 shows how our own union serves as a vehicle for building cultures of resistance, democratic organizations, and tenant power. In our movement's occupations of our housing and of public and common space, we can trace the outlines of rent abolition: the absence of landlords and real estate speculators and the presence of new kinds of relationships to housing and to each other. Chapter 5 claims the horizon of our movement as a reclamation of sovereignty over shared resources and the places we inhabit. We call this a land struggle.

This book would be impossible without the members of the LA Tenants Union, whose insight and whose bravery give meaning to anything we could write. We did not write to blaze a trail for their resistance. Instead, we have shaped this book in their wake.

As night progressed on that Fourth of July, the Los Angeles sky hazed over with smoke. We could no longer see the bursts of light emerging from South Central or Echo Park. Yet we knew they persisted, continuing deep into the night, overwhelming the ability of the repressive force of cops and the law to shut them down. A liberatory struggle is like this: sometimes you lose, and sometimes you lose your way. But we know the sparks are still there. We hope you read this book in community with others. Like fireworks, it's better shared.

CHAPTER 1

RENT IS THE CRISIS

"The tradition of the oppressed teaches us that the 'state of
emergency' in which we live is not the exception but the rule."
—Walter Benjamin

EVERY FIRST OF the month, we hand over a share of our wages to
meet our human need for housing. Our rents rise faster than our
incomes, and inequality grows. Every first of the month, more tenants go without food, medication, and basic necessities to pay this
tribute. More people take up residence with family, in cars, and in
tents outdoors. But every first of the month is another opportunity
for organizing, collective action, and collective refusal. Every first
of the month is an occasion to educate ourselves and our neighbors
about the housing system that ensnares and degrades us. Every first
of the month, we can bargain for better conditions, gain more control of how we live. Every first of the month is a chance to take a risk.

In the fairy tale of our capitalist housing system, the price of
rent results in a balanced equation of wants and needs. Rental housing, the story goes, is a product that a landlord generously provides;
tenants can make informed and unfettered decisions to select an

appropriate place; the modest profits our landlords derive are deserved compensation for the crucial service they offer; our housing is well-appointed and our tenures respected; the money earned from our jobs more than covers the cost of our rents; over time, if we are responsible with our resources, we can save up enough to exit the rental market and buy ourselves a home.

For anyone who has ever paid rent, it's obvious this isn't how it goes. By now, the statistics feel so familiar they fail to produce any sense of shock: It would take four full-time minimum-wage jobs to afford to rent a typical two-bedroom apartment anywhere in the United States.[1] Half of the 100 million tenants in the country—twenty-two million tenant households—spend more than a third of their income on rent.[2] A quarter spend over half of that income. In Los Angeles alone, 600,000 people spend fully 90 percent of what they earn keeping a roof over their heads.[3] More than 653,000 people across the country are homeless every night, the highest number recorded since the federal government began its count.[4] And every minute of the day, landlords file seven evictions—totaling 3.6 million evictions a year.[5]

The humiliating experiences of paying rent are familiar to us, too: the shame of our light fixtures swelled with rainwater, or our rice infested with roaches; the fury of watching a few rolls of paint cover that swelling black morass above our shower; the resolve to eat our child's leftovers, rather than risk a late fee; the anxiety of condensing our lives into cardboard boxes, while the sheriff paces at our door; the depression that grips us as the places where we grew up lose their texture, become no longer ours, sites of childhood memories and current community ripped up like wildflowers from a field.

These dire statistics and degrading experiences are often collected under the banner of "the housing crisis." But the capitalist housing system is working exactly as designed: to enrich land-lords, developers, and real estate speculators. In the 2010s, land-lords raked in over $4.5 trillion from tenants in rent payments.[6] In 2019 alone, those rent payments totaled $512.4 billion. As land-lording has become an irresistible way to make money, landlords have taken over more and more homes, enriching corporations and the already rich. In 2021, landlords bought nearly one in seven homes sold in the forty largest US cities—and nearly one in three homes sold in Black neighborhoods.[7] Framing the consequences of our housing system as a "housing crisis" ignores that from the perspective of its winners, the system works just fine. The capitalist housing system isn't designed to provide the best quality housing to the most tenants. It's designed to maximize profits and to extract the most rent.

Housing isn't in crisis, *tenants* are. Our lives are wrecked and wrung by price gouging, eviction, and displacement. We suffer trauma, loss, precarity, panic, poor health, and premature death. For poor and working-class people, particularly people of color, this crisis is permanent. The capitalist housing system has never provided universal access to safe and stable homes, and the policies enshrined by our federal, state, and municipal governments—both its compromised regulations and its deliberate deregulations—maintain crisis as the norm.

The frame of "housing crisis" trains our attention away from the fundamental power imbalance between landlords and tenants. It suggests that to solve the crisis, we should focus on the people who design housing, who build housing, who profit from hous-ing, not the people who live in it. It encourages us to think about abstract, interchangeable "housing units" and not about power, or about people and the constraints that shape their lives.

Why do tenants wake up every month and have to pay rent? Power, to paraphrase Frances Fox Piven and Richard Cloward, comes from control over two things: the means of extracting wealth and the means of physical coercion.[8] Landlords have both. They are empowered to take our money as rent and call on the sheriffs or cops to use force if we can't pay. The entire real estate industry relies on privatizing a common resource (land), hoarding a human need (housing), blocking public intervention or competition, and maintaining a captive market of tenants to exploit and dominate. The immiseration of tenants is a feature of a housing system built on this unequal power dynamic, not a bug we can tinker away. Tenants are exploited and oppressed not just by corporate landlords, or by unscrupulous landlords, but by the fact of having a landlord at all.

Rather than *renter*, we use the expansive term *tenant*. The concept harkens back to landlords' feudal title, which makes their power clear. It also refuses the dehumanizing division that ejects unhoused people from our analyses as soon as they are pushed from their homes. A tenant is more than a renter. A tenant is anyone who doesn't control their housing, who inhabits but doesn't own. Like the word *tent*, the origin of the word *tenant* is from the Latin *tenere*, which means "to hold" or "to have." Tenants hold space but are vulnerable to having it taken away.

Rent isn't the dispassionate outcome of supply meeting demand; it is the index of struggle between those who own or invest in housing and those who live in it. Rent is a power relation that produces inequality, traps us in poverty, and denies us the capacity to live as we choose. Rent is exploitation and domination. It separates us from our neighbors and alienates us from the places we live. It is the engine that turns a human need into a product to be exploited, bet on, and banked. Rent is the crisis. We pay the price of rent in money, but also in our dignity.[9]

In our nine years building the LA Tenants Union, we've seen the consequences of this power relation in the spectacular and the mundane, from landlords large and small: a "mom and pop" breaking down a tenant's front door with a pickax, a thousand-unit corporation issuing lies dressed up in legalese. The subject of our organizing in the union is not housing but tenants. In other words, it's us. Tenants, unlike housing, have race, gender, family, and biography. And tenants can have power. A tenant can be incarcerated, living in their car, on a couch, or in a tent outside. A tenant can be in kindergarten, can be a teacher—even a teacher on strike. A tenant can be harassed, evicted, displaced, broke, undocumented, fed up—or organized. Tenants can't afford to be passive objects of social intervention or beneficiaries of a quick "one-weird-wonky-policy" fix. It's we who must organize to wrest control over where and how we live from those who exploit and dominate us, to protect our homes and to make home a guarantee for all.

For many of us who have suffered the indignities of rent, nothing we write here will be a surprise. Every first of the month, we know something is rotten. Every first of the month, we wonder what it would take to never pay rent again. Often, our fantasies are individual: we'll get a windfall, make it big, or play our cards right, earn our way up. Sure, some of us will make it into the home-owning ranks. But most of us won't. We'll pay up, or leave town, downsize, and retreat. If we want to end the misery of rent for everyone, we'll need to trade our individualistic fantasies for universal abundance. And we'll need to work together.

We pay rent at the peril of our need and at the barrel of a gun. In this chapter, we offer a straightforward analysis of the rent relation from the perspective of tenants. We want to empower tenants to cut through the myths, misconceptions, and downright lies that hold up the system we're in, and to recognize the true insanity of what we take for granted as normal. Peeling back the underlying dynamics of rent isn't just an intellectual exercise. Armed with a shared analysis of our situation, we can decide together what to do.

What Is Rent?

All human beings need shelter. All human beings need a home. If we don't own property, we have to pay rent to meet these needs. *Rent is a fine for having a human need.* If we can't afford to buy a home, from the day we are separated from our parents or caretakers, we have no choice but to pay rent. We don't get to decide if we pay or not, and we don't get to decide how much we pay. In the absence of rent controls, landlords have complete price-setting power. Average rents have more than doubled over the last two decades, while wages have plateaued for the last four.[10] Over the last half a century, as wages stagnated and the cost of rent ballooned, we've simply paid more and more to keep our housing. We've had no other choice.

Rent is the gap between tenants' needs and landlords' demands. It benefits tenants for housing to be built to last, well maintained, easily accessible, and cheap; tenants need stability, safety, a place to live and make a life. It benefits landlords for housing to be cheaply produced, rarely maintained, scarce, and expensive; landlords seek to maximize profit, driving down costs and driving up rents. They want to take more money out and put ever less back in. This is the fundamental contradiction between the use of a home as a place to live and the use of a home as a place to extract wealth, what it means to live inside a system in which housing is something used to make a profit.

Tenants live inside the landlord's profit-maximization vise. The consequences of cost cutting are our living conditions. Mold, cold, rodents, roaches, lead, asbestos, and contaminated water are endemic to rental housing. Almost 3.9 million households in the US rent what the US Department of Housing and Urban Development classifies as "inadequate" housing, with plumbing, electrical, or heating issues, where pests thrive and our health declines.[11] The incentive to maximize returns means landlords spend the minimum to maintain our homes; after months of dodging our calls, they'd rather perform quick fixes than deep repairs, the band-aid-on-bullet-hole ethos we call "the landlord special." When our roof swells with water, we're expected to pay for the privilege of having a roof at all. When the mold makes us sick, we pay for the privilege of being poisoned.

LANDLORDS DON'T OWN our homes because they are better than us, smarter than us, or more hardworking than us. Our landlords own our homes because at some point in the past they—or their parents, or their parents' parents—had more money than us. Rent is the price of being poorer than others, of our parents being poorer than the parents of others. It's no wonder that the descendants of enslaved and Indigenous people, immigrants, and people of color are more likely to pay rent and to be unhoused.[12] (Over half of Black households pay rent to secure housing; only a third of white households do.[13]) As the feudal name "landlord" continues to suggest, *rent is a monthly tribute* to those with generational wealth, a hoard of resources built on stolen lives and stolen land.[14]

The third of Americans who rent their housing make these payments to a handful of corporations and the mere 6.7 percent of the population who own that housing. This is a transfer of wealth from over 100 million tenants to just over 11 million landlords.[15] The poorest Americans are overwhelmingly tenants; the richest own real estate.[16] *Rent is an engine of inequality.* If you've played the board game Monopoly, you understand the idea: a roll of the dice and a purchase allow you to extract rents until everyone else is bankrupt.

Tenants work; landlords live off our labor. According to 2021 US Census data, the average individual landlord spends less than four hours a month maintaining a property, while the average revenue they claim on that property is over $25,000 a month.[17] *The "passive" income of rent is active income stolen from those of us who work.*[18]

Landlords make money by extracting rent, but they also can expect to make money just by owning a piece of property. Housing is an asset; it appreciates. Simply by existing, its value goes up over time. In our current arrangement, the value of housing combines that of the physical buildings we live in and that of the land underneath. In the long term, even when those physical buildings deteriorate, the value of land only ever seems to rise.[19] As government policy subsidizes private assets and banks hand out loans, landlords and would-be homeowners bid up prices. The constant inflation of property values is locked into our system as a self-fulfilling prophecy.[20] In a "housing bubble," the bets landlords and would-be owners place on housing become a competitive frenzy, driving up prices beyond what reality can immediately bear. But the underlying dynamic of speculation remains even in so-called normal times; no matter how much homes cost now, in the not-so-long run they will cost more. Of course, the tenant sees none of the benefits of this appreciation. To pay rent is to get stuck out in the economic cold.

Here is one viral celebration of landlord math: "Bank buys me the house. Tenants pay off the loan. Property manager handles everything. I collect cash every month. Inflation builds me massive wealth. Real Estate."[21] *Rent is our money, which landlords invest for their gain.* Each month we pay not just what it costs our landlords to maintain our housing but what it costs our landlords to own an asset that makes them money over time. Their so-called expenses are minimal repairs so we don't complain, insurance so they're not on the hook if we get hurt, then the taxes and mortgage interest it requires for them to keep owning our house. Once a landlord has used our rents to pay off every cent of that mortgage, our rents don't go down; their profits go up. For the temporary inconvenience of passing on our money to their banks, landlords can charge us rent in perpetuity. The industry's "50 percent rule" encourages landlords to set rent at double those monthly costs.[22] If our landlords use that metric, each month we pay those expenses, then pay them again.

The supposed cure for renting is owning your own home. But *rent is a trap.* When tenants try to buy a house, we find that landlords already have the advantage. Tax work-arounds, special interest rates, and all-cash offers make housing effectively cheaper the more money you have, crowding us out of options.[23] Our landlords can buy more buildings just by pulling out equity from their mortgages or borrowing against the buildings they already have.[24] They can use their assets, which we pay for, to surf from debt to debt. Meanwhile, as homes get more expensive and further out of reach, tenants are compelled to keep renting for a longer period of time. The longer we rent, the further we are from saving enough to compete. Paying rent is keeping us from reaching the first rung of that imagined "property ladder." And our lost ground is our landlords' gain.[25] Our rents don't just vanish when we send in our checks. They pay off our landlords' mortgages, so they can claim their second (or fourth, or hundredth) house.[26] When people say paying rent is like "throwing money in the trash," they're only half right; it's our trash can, but our landlord's bank account.

Landlord lobbyists have crusaded to rebrand themselves as "housing providers" and rid themselves of the feudal title that makes their power clear, but landlords do not "provide" housing, they extract rent from housing by hoarding the places where we can live.[27] When our rents are leveraged for more housing grabs, landlords take over more and more space.[28] Already-wealthy people, corporations, and financial firms profit; more of us are tenants than ever before.[29] *Rent is an engine of consolidation.* It drives the ownership of housing into fewer and fewer hands.[30] In 2013, Invitation Homes issued the first-ever rent-backed security with 3,200 homes in its portfolio.[31] Just ten years later, the company now owns more than 80,000 homes nationwide. Its business model turns rents into securities to sell to investors, so they can buy up more homes, and start over again.

Of course, Invitation Homes generates those rents through the classic profit-maximization strategy of hiked prices and forced-down costs: between 2014 and 2016, the company raised average rents in its portfolio from $1,424 to $1,600 a month, while its *yearly* maintenance expenditures per unit shrunk from $1,362 to $1,146.[32] And tenants experience the consolidation of our landlords in more than money. Large corporate landlords are more likely to evict us or threaten us with eviction, to raise our rents every year, and to gouge us with fines and fees—pet rents, landscaping costs, utility mark-ups, smart-home subscriptions, even legal fees for their illegal eviction notices.[33]

RENT PREVENTS US from caring for ourselves and each other. What do tenants do when landlords hike up our rents? We double up.[34] More than 370,000 families in LA alone live in overcrowded homes, stunting our children's development and putting us at greater risk of dying in apartment fires or outbreaks of disease.[35] We stay in violent partnerships because we can't afford to leave.[36] We starve and sacrifice our health. In 2019, 30 percent of tenants nationwide were food insecure, and 20 percent had an unmet medical need, because they'd prioritized paying rent.[37] This is tenant math: skimping on basic necessities and jeopardizing our safety to pay for our homes. As the saying goes, rent eats first.[38]

Landlords know they control access to a basic survival need. Blackstone's CEO Stephen Schwarzman has celebrated the housing market for its "complete control." Frank Rolfe of RV Horizons compared his mobile home parks to "a Waffle House where the customers are chained to the booths."[39] Just for the privilege of paying rent, we pay application fees; subject ourselves to credit checks; jump over or squeeze into income requirements; swallow restrictions on pets, roommates, and family members; suffer source-of-income, racial, ethnic, and homophobic discrimination; fork over exorbitant broker fees and deposits; and expose our conviction and eviction history. We accept harsh leases, dilapidated living conditions, gouged rents. Why? Because *behind each rent check is the threat of homelessness.*[40] Landlords' control over our access to the indoors pushes us to accept degrading living conditions and degrading terms.

Behind each rent check is the threat of eviction. When landlords risk losing money and tenants risk losing a home, our housing system rules in their favor, no matter the social cost. US evictions nearly doubled between 2000 and 2016.[41] The most common reason tenants are evicted? We can't pay the rent.[42] In LA, from just February to November 2023, landlords filed 71,429 eviction notices, nonpayment the cause of 96 percent.[43] And across the country, Black tenants receive evictions at nearly twice the rate of white ones.[44] These statistics don't even include "informal evictions" of tenants kicked out without a legal process, sometimes through violence; "constructive evictions" of tenants driven out by unlivable conditions; or "polite evictions" of tenants who are effectively evicted by nonrenewed leases or legal rent increases they can't afford.[45] But the scarlet letter of an eviction, or just an appearance in court, can strap us with debt, bar us from jobs, degrade our health, and make it harder to get housing again.

Behind each rent check is the threat of state violence. If we can't pay the rent, or if we defy any terms our landlords set, they can call on deputies of the state to throw us out of our homes. A deed is a voucher for state violence.[46] When a landlord calls in that right, the state will do the dirty work of physical force for them, sending its officers to evict. Every form of communication, from a pay-or-quit notice to a bullying text, from an unannounced visit to a shoddy repair, bears the mark of that threat. In verbal harassment, physical intimidation, even assault, in withheld services or building repairs, the landlord pantomimes the power of violence vested in them by the sheriff and the state.[47]

RENT IS THE *private capture of public investment.* It's often said that only three things matter in real estate: location, location, location. What this betrays is how exactly landlords extract rent from place. It's not just the building they own, but where the building is, that makes housing more or less valuable. The value of a location is often shaped by our bosses, that is, by where and how we are forced to work a wage. But rent doesn't just steal from the wages we earn as individuals, it steals from the value the public creates. We know this intuitively: proximity to parks and recreation, to good schools, to transit stops make housing cost more; centrally located apartments can claim higher rents. But each of these reflects the quality of the neighborhood, not just the quality of the building: public, not private investment.

"All housing is public housing," as David Madden and Peter Marcuse put it.[48] Public investment is a precondition for private profit. Even what we think of as privately owned housing relies on vast public infrastructure to exist. That physical infrastructure includes the pipes that deliver water, the sewers that carry out waste, the sidewalks, roads, and transportation systems that connect our housing to our neighborhoods and our neighborhoods to each other. Public infrastructure also means legal and financial systems, from the contracts that govern leases, to the regulations that dictate everything from what counts as a bedroom to the terms of financing loans. The private housing market could not exist without the support of the state. When a city invests in a new subway stop or expands zoning restrictions so landowners can build, the value of locations rise. Landlords claim this value that the public creates for themselves, extracting it from tenants in the form of higher rents.

Rent steals the common labor of tenants, who create the communities where they live. From neighborhood safety achieved by self-organization, to paths of desire that produce local culture, to the public rituals of street life, to volunteer efforts that beautify public space, tenants, together, make their neighborhoods what they are. It was Black tenants who made Harlem the epicenter of American culture in 1920s New York, queer tenants who made the 1960s' Castro in San Francisco a mecca of militancy, and Mexican mariachi musicians who gave the Boyle Heights plaza where they still work its name. Our neighborhoods are made by the tenants who live in them.[49] By creating communities and inhabiting the places we live, tenants produce the value of our neighborhoods. But it's landlords who can leverage that value as the passive income of rent.

Rent relies on the state abandonment of tenants. "Can you afford to pay your neighbor's rent?" asked a 1933 industry campaign against public housing. But tenants subsidize the wealth of their neighbors—or absentees—our tax dollars paying off our neighbors' mortgages. The federal government spends at least three times as much on subsidizing homeowners than it does on tenant support.[50] (And since a homeowner has a full forty times the net worth of a tenant, that's three times more subsidies for those least in need.[51])

Rent metabolizes racism. Racism has long fueled real estate greed, just as real estate greed has made race what it is today. The exclusion of people of color from certain neighborhoods made homes more valuable: white buyers paid a premium for keeping them out. And the containment of people of color in other neighborhoods made rents higher there, too: Black and Brown tenants were forced to pay a premium; they were trapped in segregated markets from which it was impossible to leave.[52] Past and present appraisals of property value incorporate racist calculations of whose lives, whose homes, and whose neighborhoods have worth.

Racist exclusion from homeownership (by local deed restrictions or federal redlining) or inclusion only under predatory terms (from rent-to-own to subprime schemes) created the six-to-one white–Black racial wealth gap and a dual housing market in which the majority of people of color are tenants and the majority of white people own their homes.[53] And though legal segregation was struck down, housing discrimination endures via the proxies of credit scores, home size, income, and eviction, incarceration, or arrest histories. "There has not been an instance in the last 100 years when the housing market has operated fairly, without racial discrimination," Keeanga-Yamahtta Taylor writes.[54] And not an instance when landlords and real estate developers didn't leverage discrimination for profit.

RENT PRODUCES UNEQUAL, *disfigured cities.* One business model of rent is trapping tenants in poverty, then exploiting the captive market of the poor. The margins are extreme. Landlords can extract almost twice the profits from tenants in poor neighborhoods as they can from those in rich ones. In places where more than half of residents live in poverty, a landlord can get back every penny of what they paid to buy a building in just four years of collecting rent.[55] In 1992, Mike Davis dubbed the Los Angeles suburb of Bell Gardens a "rent plantation," where rents from Latinx immigrants were wrung by white absentees.[56] The upward transfer of rent perpetuates segregation: resources are extracted from poor neighborhoods to circulate within rich ones. We see the results of this segregation etched into space: some neighborhoods with well-lit streets lined with shade trees, regular trash pickup, and public schools with iPads; others with uncovered bus stops, potholes, and rats.

Rent deprives us of agency over where we live. Rent sorts us by quality of housing and its location: since rent prices determine who gets to live where, the poor are condemned to the worst housing in the least desirable locations, while central districts can be guarded as elite pleasure domes. We get stuck in neighborhoods we can't afford to leave, then expelled from those places as soon as landlords can move richer tenants in. Rent means we get contained and segregated or displaced and replaced. Rent both traps us in place and pushes us out.[57]

If a capitalist firm and a landlord had a baby, it'd be a developer. Real estate developers seek to drive down costs—of building materials and the labor it takes to build a new home or apartment block. But unlike manufacturers of TVs, cars, and refrigerators, they don't pass these savings on to us. They have no need to: they can capture the distance between inflating property values and our dire need.[58] Like landlords, real estate developers don't "provide" housing, they speculate on it. Real estate developers can only raise funds on the basis of future profits; they plan for high rents. Their output is tied to market booms and busts. They invest in, produce, and profit from scarcity; they modulate the flow of new housing to ensure it remains. And they share with landlords and homeowners a fundamental material interest in ensuring that land and property values only ever continue to rise—a lock-in of rents ever going up.

Securing housing doesn't mean competing just with other people who want to use it to live in. It means competing with people and corporations who want to use it to make money. More than 68 percent of the world's wealth is held in real estate, and 79 percent of that is in residential housing. In 2020, the total residential real estate value in the US—the second-largest share in the world—amounted to $258.5 trillion: that's more valuable than all global equities and debt securities combined, more than twenty times more valuable than all the gold ever mined.[59] To speak in the language of supply and demand, the price of housing is not determined just by local demand for housing, but by the global search for opportunities to seek profit.[60] *The housing market doesn't produce homes, it produces opportunities for investment.*

Real estate speculation produces strategic disinvestment and overdevelopment. When property owners decide that a property is worth more empty or demolished than it is inhabited, they leave that property uninhabited, allow it to rot. Busted windows, dilapidated roofs, and vacant buildings result. But overdevelopment produces vacancy, too. When the rich buy property as a pied-à-terre, Airbnb rental, or investment scheme, we get vacant apartments as luxury blight. A $2.3 billion luxury apartment and retail complex, Ocean-wide Plaza, has now stood abandoned in downtown LA for five years, just blocks from Skid Row. The scandal of vacant housing beside people without homes made national headlines when graffiti artists claimed the half-built building as a canvas. The city allocated $3.8 million to secure the site.[61] This is one of the starkest examples of the contradiction of rent: homes sit empty while people lack homes.

RENT MEANS SOME *people won't have housing.* The need for housing is equal and universal: everyone needs it, and no one deserves it more than anyone else. But having to pay for housing means only those who can afford it get to have it at all. As rents rise, so do the ranks of unhoused tenants. Across the country, a $100 increase in median rent means a 9 percent increase in homelessness.[62] But homeless-ness isn't an equal-opportunity misery; it tracks people into life outcomes along grooves worn by enslavement and inequality. Black people are 13 percent of the US population but 37 percent of those who sleep outdoors.[63]

If we're caught without a home, we can be subjected to police harassment, brutality, tickets, or jail. That is, *it's illegal to not pay rent.* Across 187 cities, the number of bans on putting up tents, living in cars, asking passersby for money, and resting or even *being* in public just about doubled between 2006 and 2019.[64] The widespread crim-inalization of living in public space means that we don't just have to pay rent because we need housing. We have to pay rent because it's a crime not to have it.

A threat of eviction makes us more likely to die in the next twenty years; an eviction judgment doubles that likelihood to 40 percent. Even high rents predict mortality: the higher our rent burdens, the sooner and likelier our deaths.[65] Of course, the risks are worse when we live outdoors. The life expectancy of an unhoused person is just 48 years, an average of 30 years cut short. It is not an exaggeration to say *rent kills*.[66] Housing—and unhousing—is a matter of life and death.

Tenant Power

Home is an inescapable need for every person. Home organizes our lives, from the families we do and don't choose, to the ability to hold down work, to the coincidences that end up making us who we are. Our most personal sorrows and private joys, our invitations to the many forms of intimacy we experience, good and bad, are mediated by where we live. We sleep, we eat, we shit, we fuck, we call our moms. We care for our sick grandparents. We rest, relax, zone out. We wonder how we'll make it work another day. Everyone needs home, so everyone deserves one. Rent is standing in our way.

Our capitalist housing system sorts who among us is exposed to environmental harms, who can access a decent job or a decent hospital, who is subject to police harassment and imprisonment, who lives indoors and who outside—who lives and who dies. Designed to protect and expand the wealth of homeowners, landlords, and speculators, the system exploits and oppresses tenants. We might even call it an *un*-housing system, designed so that some of us will have nowhere to live but public space.

IN THE AFTERMATH of the 2008 financial collapse, driven by real estate greed, a renewed focus on the housing crisis did not emphasize the living conditions of the poor, but rather the rising insecurity of the middle and upper-middle classes, for whom decent and secure housing had been understood as birthrights. The proposed solution? Unleash the cranes. Since housing is scarce, goes the refrain, more private development would increase supply, driving down rents and raising tenants' respective power.

It's true that there is a shortage—of *cheap* housing.[67] Tenants are in dire need of more dwelling space that we can actually afford. Across the country, there are only 33 homes for every 100 tenant households who live in poverty. Between 1990 and 2017, about eleven million new dwellings were built nationwide, but the number affordable to poor and working-class people decreased by nearly four million.[68]

Studies of new private development's effects show mixed results. In the area immediately surrounding new construction, rents do fall for the most expensive homes, but they often go up for the rest of us.[69] Rich tenants gain lease-signing bonuses and complimentary gyms; poor tenants must wait for benefits to trickle down. At the regional scale, in the long term, tenants may "sort" themselves into new spots—sometimes a euphemism for uprooting ourselves or getting forcibly displaced. Then, new development does help slow down the insane pace of rent increases overall, giving tenants relief from the squeeze. However, new development does not stop or reverse rent's total upward march.[70] Perhaps the best critique of the just-build-more perspective is their own best-case scenario: these efforts do not produce *lower* rents, but rather rents that *rise less quickly*.[71]

Those taken by the fantasy of private construction as *the* solution to the misery of tenants believe that one side of real estate capital will compete with another: developers, who can increase supply, will join forces with tenants in the fight against landlords and homeowners, who benefit when supply is restricted. Yet private developers deliver predominantly high-end housing.[72] In times of economic downturn, they don't build anything at all.[73]

Theirs is a view of tenant power as a by-product of market forces: like a low unemployment rate, which gives workers more leverage, incentivizing bosses to improve conditions and raise pay, a higher vacancy rate would give tenants more choice, motivating landlords to make repairs and ease rent increases. But just as a tight labor market has never eliminated deadly jobs or poverty wages, a slack housing market will not eradicate slum housing or rent gouging. Indeed, it was organized labor unions that won wage floors, weekends, and safety regulations; no basic worker protection or benefit has been handed over as a gift from "job creators."

If we focus our lens on housing shortage, "housing providers" can be anointed as tenants' saviors. But this is not just a shortage; it's deliberate, strategic, even permanent scarcity—engineered famine. Already in 1872, Friedrich Engels understood: "The so-called housing shortage . . . is not something peculiar to the present. . . . All oppressed classes in all periods suffered more or less uniformly from it."[74] When we finally look at the problem on our own terms as tenants, what is revealed? This is not a broken housing market but a whole, rigged *unhousing* system. It fracks tenants' wages and keeps us vulnerable, frightened, and broke. It lines the pockets of landlords and real estate speculators as they monopolize more and more homes.

Neither building nor, for that matter, blocking new private housing will overcome the misery and injustice of rent. We need to transform the power relations that keep this system in place. We need to break the private monopoly on development—its strangle-hold over the pace and type of production, determined by profit-ability and not by our needs. We need to break the private monopoly of landlords over pieces of the earth—the hoarding of human shelter that ensures they can extract rent from us and evict us at their will. We need to dismantle the institutions of state violence, which empower the real estate industry to draw profit from a fundamental human need.

The housing crisis is not a problem to be solved; it is a class struggle to be fought and won. The conclusion that Engels drew still applies now: "In order to make an end to *this* housing short-age there is only one means: to abolish altogether the exploitation and oppression of the working class by the ruling class."[75] Rent is a fundamental engine of inequality and injustice, a transfer of wealth from the poorest to the richest, the most vulnerable to the least, which drives millions into debt and despair and onto the streets. From the perspective of tenants, the answer to the housing crisis is as simple as it is revolutionary: a world without landlords and a world without rent. Our self-interest as tenants isn't just fixing the leak in our shower; it's dismantling the capitalist unhousing system.

To overcome the crushing dynamic of *landlord* and *tenant math*, we need *movement math*. If a tenant is anyone who doesn't control their own housing, the tenant movement is our means to take collective control over where and how we live. How can we get rid of the exploitation and domination of rent? How do we make investing in housing—that is, betting on tenant misery—a riskier bet? We have to use our own power—tenant power—to change our conditions ourselves, use the few rights we have to get the rights we need.

Opportunity is knocking on your neighbor's door. In our own apartment buildings, we have to organize to constrain our landlords' powers to extract our wages as their profits, and to throw us out of our homes. By joining with our immediate neighbors to form *tenants associations*—units of tenant power at a building scale—we have to win repairs and concessions, change our landlords' equations of profit and costs, and demand that more of our rents get reinvested in our quality of life. We have to bargain for better leases, even strike for lower rents. We have to cut off the upward flow of our resources and stabilize our lives.

Beyond our own buildings, if we want to slow down the consolidation of housing and throw sand in the gears of the displacement machine, we must build larger organizations, vehicles for our building-level fights to connect and grow. A *tenants union* is the unit of tenant power at the scale of a city. We have to teach each other strategies of direct action, rent withholding, and collective bargaining. We have to support each other's actions and draw more tenants into our work. We have to build lasting, truly democratic infrastructures based on relationships of mutual care, trust, and solidarity—these are the social means for survival and for political struggle. They help us claim small victories, build new leadership, and grow our organizations, such that new possibilities emerge.

Only those policies toxic to real estate speculation can help us thrive. Unlike landlords, developers, and homeowners, tenants want and need rents—thus property values—to fall. There is no reason to shy away from the truth that what benefits tenants makes housing less profitable: it helps us clarify our interests and what criteria we should use to evaluate reforms.[76]

At the scale of our cities and nationwide, we have to press for public competition with private housing: permanent, unsurveilled, well-resourced public housing, the kind that has never been allowed to exist. Leveraging the vast capacities of the state to provide for tenants' human needs, directing public resources to the public good, public housing addresses housing as infrastructure. Expanding public housing raises the floor for every tenant by blunting the force of market pressures across the sector—that's why the real estate industry considers it such a threat.

While we struggle for public provision and common ownership, we have to win new regulations of the private market. We need controls on rent increases and even rollbacks of rents. We need limits on landlords' despotic power: bans on evictions and protections—with real enforcement mechanisms—that guarantee decent conditions. We need new mechanisms to evict our landlords, to remove our own buildings from private ownership and get them into our hands. In the context of the asset-inflating American dream, to capture the state's powers of taxation, regulation, housing provision, and eminent domain will mean to run the state against its grain. It will take mass, independent organization that understands policy outcomes as way stations of tenant power.

We need to put class conflict at the center of the housing question, and the housing question at the center of class conflict. Workers have often been the focus of this fight, but tenants (both working and unemployed) have a crucial role to play too. Exploitation through our housing has long ensured exploitation at our workplaces.[77] (Said one studio executive during the 2023 Writers Guild of America strike: "The endgame is to allow things to drag on until union members start losing their apartments."[78]) And more and more, as we've seen above, our homes are the places where our bosses park their money and where that money goes to make more of itself.[79] Tenants can be key political subjects, the architects of a long-term project of expropriation through which that hoarded wealth becomes shared by us all.[80]

Truly abolishing rent will take a mass revolutionary movement, capable of withholding rent and occupying our homes, of
overturning property relations and of transforming the state. That
movement will require us to organize as tenants where we live and
as workers where we work. It will take dense, militant organizations
along every single axis that defines our lives: public sector workers
reclaiming state resources for a robust social wage, now strip mined
for the appreciation of privately owned homes; women and queer
and trans people protecting bodily autonomy, undoing the home
as a site of control; Black radical movements for reparations, winning land redistribution promised during Reconstruction; as well
as international liberation struggles for migration and against colonial domination. We are far from that horizon, but it can serve as
our North Star.

THE ABOLITION OF rent is the absence of landlords and the presence of new relationships to housing and each other. Freedom *from*
landlords and real estate speculators is freedom *to* organize a housing system according to our needs and desires.[81] Tenants do not just
want better housing, we want better lives. We want to live with dignity, in conditions that support us in the fullness of our lives. We
want to live with power, to decide what happens to our homes, our
neighborhoods, and our cities. Unburdened by the fear of making
rent, what could we do with life's most precious resource, our time
on this earth? What could our cities be like, not as monuments to
capital and the lucky rich few, but as testaments to the many, and
the many lives we could lead?

If we want to build the kind of housing we need, socialize the
private housing we already have, win true sovereignty over our

work and its purpose, our homes and their meanings, our cities and all cities, we have to organize. Of course, organizing against rent often involves risk—to our stability, our safety, our sense of ourselves. But by not organizing we are already taking a risk, a risk that we will have to live with this housing system for the rest of our lives.

CHAPTER 2

THE WAR ON TENANTS

"In our time all politics is about real estate."
—Fredric Jameson

IN OCTOBER 2022, an anonymous source leaked an hour-long recording of three LA city councilmembers trading expletives, insults, and racist slurs about their colleagues and constituents. Black, Oaxacan, Korean, Jewish, Armenian, poor, and unhoused people were made special targets for ridicule: "shoeless," "dark," "ugly," "cocoa," those from the "village," and those with nowhere "to shit." At the time it was recorded, the council—a fifteen-member body tasked with representing nearly four million people—was in the middle of redrawing its electoral map. The recording captured the council members divvying up economic assets and conspiring to gerrymander districts. Their goal? To undermine the power of tenants.[1] "It serves us not to give [councilmember Nithya Raman] all of K-Town," said former council president Nury Martinez, "because that solidifies her renters' district, and that is not a good thing for any of us."

It shouldn't take another scandal to reveal their priorities. Four other LA city councilmembers have faced criminal charges for accepting bribes from real estate developers in as many years. Since 2005, the council has approved over $1 billion in tax breaks for new real estate projects; the homeless population has more than doubled in just seven years.[2] The leak provided a candid portrait of Democratic politics in a one-party city in a one-party state: politicians in the act of suppressing tenant power and courting real estate speculation at the expense of the residents they claim to serve. Connecting the councilmembers' racist speech to the racist practice of class domination, the tape exposed the central fault line of power in the city, between tenants on the one hand, and, on the other, an alliance of real estate and the state.

LIKE THE ROACHES in our kitchen that point to an infestation behind our walls, our individual tenant crises are part of a larger pattern of tenant disempowerment: a housing system bent into shape by the power of real estate. If rent is a power relation, then the price of rent is also an index of state regulation and deregulation, its refusals and incentives. Landlords can continue to exploit and dominate tenants because they are empowered to do so by government policy. The private housing market is shaped by the invisible hand of the state.

The history of housing policy in the twentieth century is often told as the story of the democratization of homeownership, the ongoing expansion of access to private, asset-based wealth and security. But tenants have a story too. It is a story of abandonment, exploitation, and stigmatization—a systematic assault. Just as the US government has waged wars on the poor and people of color in the guise of the "war on drugs" and the "war on crime," it has also waged a war on tenants with the same results: impoverishing, exploiting, and even criminalizing them.

The war on tenants has rigged the American housing system to benefit homeowners, landlords, and real estate speculators at the expense of tenants' human needs. On the one hand, state action has shaped our housing system to inflate property values and thus raise rents. On the other hand, it has abandoned tenants to the predation of private landlords. Excluded from the social, economic, and political benefits of homeownership, tenants have been maintained as a captive market to exploit. Race is fundamental to this process: property value animates racial categories at the same time it ensures the persistence of historical racial inequalities. Violence is also fundamental to this process: upholding and producing property value relies on legal and extralegal force. Just as dispossession of land has been a longstanding form of racist violence, racist violence remains a central tool of real estate rule.

Of course, property ownership was bloody from the start. The US regime of land ownership was specifically established for the purpose of annexing native territory, conscripting individual Americans as settlers by guaranteeing them the right to own the land they seized.[3] US property was founded upon state-sanctioned dispossession and the genocide that killed 95 percent of Indigenous populations.[4] Similarly, property ownership was defined by the legal institution of chattel slavery, with a legacy that persisted even after its defeat, as new forms of property titles—as well as formal police forces—emerged to counter Black land struggle during the aborted project of Reconstruction.[5]

Shaped in turns by racism and the red scare, our property laws and housing policies bear the marks of this history. They recognize individual claims over common ones (land owned by someone, rather than everyone), prioritize extractive over subsistence use (what can make the most money from property not what can enable the most people to survive), and exclude based on racial categories. From the containment of populations on reservations and into prisons, to segregation that orders access to space by race, housing has long been a tool of population management, repression, and control.

One Hundred Years of Real Estate Rule

The concerted war on tenants over the last century shapes the current terrain of tenant struggle. Our account of this war begins in the Great Depression, when president Herbert Hoover reminded his constituents, the majority of whom paid rent to secure housing: "Those immortal ballads, 'Home, Sweet Home,' 'My Old Kentucky Home' and the 'Little Gray Home in the West' were not written about tenements or apartments. . . . They never sang songs about a pile of rent receipts."[6]

Already, as commerce secretary, Hoover had praised homeownership as "the foundation of a solid economic and social system" and collaborated with the National Association of Realtors to promote it as the civic duty of the "real American."[7] But by 1933, the calamity of the Great Depression had pushed a quarter of the workforce into unemployment and over one million people into homelessness.[8] One thousand homes were foreclosed on every day.[9] "Hooverville" encampments of informal structures proliferated in public space. Yet the one-term president responded to this crisis by creating the first federal subsidy that aided banks in offering home loans, which only benefited would-be homeowners. Tenants, figuratively and literally, were left out in the cold.

Working-class organization channeled the widespread unrest of this era into a meaningful threat to the capitalist order, securing ambitious housing reforms from Hoover's successor, Franklin D. Roosevelt. Roosevelt's New Deal cemented a bifurcated system, with enduring entitlements for homeowners and stigmatized support for tenants, vulnerable to attack. For the former group, it created new financial tools, including the fixed-rate, thirty-year mortgage; new guarantees on loans that eased banks' ability to offer them; and new bureaucracies for real estate administration, often staffed by industry professionals. These policies anointed a new generation of homeowners and solidified the subordinate status of tenants, who were systematically denied those privileges.

Race was a central axis of this exclusion. Segregation was the real estate industry's official policy. The realtor association's Code of Ethics, in effect from 1924 to 1974, insisted its members must "never be instrumental in introducing into a neighborhood . . . members of any race or nationality, or any individuals whose presence will clearly be detrimental to property values."[10] Those borders were maintained by force and by law—both through vigilante violence and the policing of neighborhoods where people of color lived.

The government standardized an appraisal system for property values that enshrined the real estate industry's racist evaluations of people of color. Ex–real estate broker and Federal Housing Administration (FHA) director Homer Hoyt drafted a national rubric of loan-underwriting criteria—a "ranking of races and nationalities with respect to their beneficial effect upon land values."[11] That appraisal system ranked English, German, and Scandinavian immigrants and their descendants first, then Italians and Jews— identified as communist sympathizers prone to rent strikes—then Black people, and finally, Mexicans.[12]

The real estate industry relied on numerous techniques to shut out people of color: restrictive deeds, which barred them from owning homes in white neighborhoods; redlining, which denied them access to mortgages (or saddled them with subpar terms); and exclusionary zoning, which barred them by proxy by prohibiting the construction of multifamily apartments.[13] Thus, the product that real estate and the state collaborated to create was not just housing, it was segregated housing. Its exclusions made it valuable.[14] Prejudice was profitable.

Slums made money, too. Barred from the social, economic, and political benefits of homeownership, tenants were a captive market, subject to mortifying conditions, exorbitant prices, and unstable housing. Residential churn was a part of life, and tenants had no other choice but to accept the terms and pay the rent. Indeed, the legal contracts of leases were governed by the standard of "caveat emptor," which until the 1970s made tenants responsible for rent payments no matter the condition of their homes.[15]

The New Deal also made a lasting impact on tenants' lives, creating the first federal public housing projects, where some would finally be (and still are) spared the predation of the private market. But the real estate industry's attacks deferred the dream of well-appointed, mixed-income tenant communities with a reality of stigmatization and decline. Concessions including caps on per-unit investment and restrictions that allowed only the poorest to qualify starved public housing of resources, ensured buildings would physically deteriorate, and established a consensus that a public option would always mean inferior housing.[16] Laws empowered local governments to veto projects or segregate them to the least desirable areas. One-to-one stipulations that tethered production of new dwellings to the destruction of slums bludgeoned the impact of public supply on private rents.

To protect their right to profit from housing, the industry consistently framed their attacks as a defense against communism.

Robert Gerholz, president of the National Home Builders, threatened that public housing would allow the US to "be precipitated
into a socialist state."[17] The industry and its elected allies recognized that housing shapes the population: it creates kinds of workers, consumers, and citizens. In the common spaces of apartments,
tenants might forge solidarity and have a stake in shared well-being;
isolated and disciplined by debt, however, the homeowner would
preside over his individualist kingdom. As Hoyt once put it, "Communism can never win in a nation of homeowners."[18] By blocking a
guarantee to a dignified home regardless of tenants' ability to pay,
the real estate industry forced most tenants to turn to the private
market.

WORLD WAR II reorganized the economy and geography of the country. By the 1940s, pushed by Jim Crow and pulled by employment in
war industries, more than six million Black people relocated to urban
centers. US government guest-worker programs also spurred immigration from Central and South America—a fair-weather reversal of
the deportation project that had ejected two million Mexicans just
a decade before. LA's population of Black residents nearly doubled.
But interlocking real estate exclusions restricted the places Black
and Brown people could live to just 5 percent of the area of the city.[19]
When new residents met segregation there and across the country,
the consequence was overcrowding, excessive rents, and landlords
with little incentive to improve dank apartments, dark garages,
leaky basements, and informal shacks. As one New York City judge
described the plight of new Black residents, "We have extended to
them the privilege of paying the highest rents for the rottenest roosts
out of the poorest wages for the dirtiest jobs."[20]

But the need to stabilize working populations for the war effort inspired national regulation in the form of rent control. In 1942, the Office of Price Administration (OPA), empowered by the war to hold down prices on food, gasoline, and other necessary goods, instituted patchwork controls for rent as well. This included protections from eviction and rent gouging as well as funding for local rent offices, where tenants often enforced controls through enthusiastic complaints, one contract at a time.[21]

Relief was short-lived, as landlords demanded that rent control be rolled back, then altogether scrapped. Conservative agitation continued to stymie public housing and ensure that a shortage of cheap apartments would outlast caps on rent. Racism and anticommunism proved a potent amalgam. One member of the South Los Angeles Homeowners Association synthesized anti-Black racism and prejudice against the alleged communist proclivities of Jews plainly in 1943 by complaining, "All these goddamn New York Jews are coming here to put the n——s in our neighborhood."[22] The real estate industry seized on local bigotry and local levers of power to veto federal public housing plans. In Los Angeles, by 1952, they had won forty out of sixty local referenda to block projects and managed to slash the city's federal contract by nearly 60 percent. The resulting landscape was, in historian Don Parson's words, "the spatial expression of the Red Scare."[23]

POSTWAR ECONOMIC RECOVERY centered around public investment in homeownership and the mass consumption it inspired. The 1944 GI Bill's zero-down home loans, which privileged new construction, lured homeowners into freshly speculated suburbs. Developers flipped rural land into single-family houses, which families filled with a record number of fridges and washing machines, and traveled to and from in a record number of cars.[24] As historian Dolores Hayden insists, the built environment of the suburbs kicked off an unending cycle of private consumption and cemented a patriarchal division of labor: women were isolated to cooking, cleaning, and care and made dependent on a husband's wage.[25] Subject to local vetoes and requiring the support of private mortgages, the GI Bill actively subsidized white flight. Real estate professionals capitalized on racist fears that linked the presence of people of color to declining property values through a tactic called "blockbusting." As one agent boastfully described it, "I specialize in locating blocks which I consider ripe for racial change . . . I make my money—and quite a lot of it incidentally—in three ways: 1) by beating down the prices I pay the white owners . . . 2) by selling to the eager Negroes at inflated prices; and 3) by financing these purchases at what amounts to a very high rate of interest."[26] Of course, this process drove further real estate gains: panicked demand for suburban homes.

Suburbanization flipped the nation from a tenant to a homeowner majority. In less than two decades, more than twenty-seven million white people relocated to the suburbs, fleeing integration and chasing government subsidies.[27] There, they used their outsized political influence to shore up segregation with an expansive toolkit of deed restrictions and local zoning regulations. As one real estate lobbyist bragged, "We helped think up the idea of city zoning ordinances."[28] (To this day, on three-quarters of developable land in the United States, only single-family homes can be built.[29]) Suburban homeowners traded public transit, parks, and social support for private cars, yards, and property values. They evacuated cities of resources by withdrawing from urban tax bases, even as they continued to depend on the same cities for jobs and infrastructure.

They were recruited into alignment with the real estate regime: private asset inflation over public good.

In the cities, landlords let dwellings crumble. Many were overcrowded, black with soot from shoddy furnaces, and lacking running water, toilets, or showers.[30] Truman's 1949 Housing Act had promised more: "a decent home and a suitable living environment for every American family" through 810,000 new public apartments and the eradication of urban slums. But with public housing choked at the local level, cities followed through on only the second of these mandates. The act's slum clearance provisions expanded local powers of eminent domain, subsidized the acquisition and demolition of land no matter its current use, and introduced a new beneficiary of this process: private enterprise. Residential and commercial developers could claim the land that governments cleared; real estate had won the power not only to contain and gouge urban populations, but to remove them.[31]

The displacement of more than a thousand Latinx families from LA's La Loma, Bishop, and Palo Verde, now often called Chavez Ravine, dramatizes this process acutely.[32] Those predominantly Mexican American neighborhoods of self-built housing had thrived for decades until the city sought the land. From 1951 to 1959, officials duped residents with undervalued buyouts, condemned their homes as blight, and finally expelled them by force.[33] The dispossessions were carried out to clear the site for a public housing project, but those homes were never built, killed by a mayor elected to block "un-American" public housing.[34] The evicted residents would not return. In 1957, the constitutional mandate that the land be used for a "public purpose" was finally fulfilled through a $1 deal with a private investor. He'd build a baseball stadium to lure Brooklyn's Dodgers to LA.

From 1949 to 1974, the United States redeveloped over 550 square miles of urban land and displaced 300,000 households, up to 1.2 million people.[35] A twenty-seven-lane confluence of six different freeways tore through LA's Boyle Heights. A single interchange, which residents still call the "spaghetti bowl," pushed out at least 10,000 mostly Latinx people. Across the country, two-thirds of those displaced by blight-and-switch schemes were renters, and 55 percent were Black.[36] Housing outcomes subjected Black and Brown people to different forms of exploitation that compounded across time and marked populations as deserving of discrimination; they made race have meaning.[37]

Real estate racism fueled the uprisings of the late sixties: Watts, Harlem, Newark, and Detroit, most famously, but also Rochester, Philadelphia, Dayton, Atlanta, Buffalo, Kansas City, Pittsburgh, Louisville, Waterloo. Nationwide, 960 cities and towns erupted in open rebellion.[38] When President Johnson tasked the Kerner Commission with identifying the root cause of the riots, their final report noted three central themes: poverty, police brutality, and housing. Confirming what many called the "race tax," housing cost Black people more, but was three times as likely to be both overcrowded and substandard. "White society is deeply implicated in the ghetto," the authors wrote. "White institutions created it, white institutions maintain it, and white society condones it."[39] The fact had been observed a decade earlier by writer and revolutionary autoworker James Boggs, who compared the ring of absentee ownership that surrounded Black neighborhoods—rent gouging residents and neglecting maintenance—to a white noose.[40] And even when the Supreme Court struck down explicit discrimination, the proxies of home size, income, and property value itself preserved the effect.[41]

Of course, conditions of overcrowding, dilapidation, and over-policing were also endemic to newly expanding immigrant communities. US-sponsored civil wars and US trade–induced poverty had drawn Latinx migrants to US urban centers, just in time to make up the gaps left by white flight.[42] In New York, the Puerto Rican militants of the Young Lords responded to urban abandonment with a daylong occupation of a disinvested city hospital and a "garbage offensive," in which they collected trash in their neighborhood and lit it ablaze in the streets, winning resources for their community.[43] In LA, where the Latinx population would soon surpass the white one, high school students leading the Chicanx Blowouts drew concessions for the city's failing public school system.[44]

Tenants tried to claw back resources by controlling their rents. Mobilizations of the sixties and seventies drew a wave of rent-stabilization ordinances across 170 municipalities, mostly in California and the Northeast. More moderate than controls, stabilization allowed steady rent increases, permanent exemptions for new construction, and loopholes to kick down the cost of repairs, but it was still a victory. These were collective bargaining agreements between landlords and tenants at the city scale.[45] "Today we control rent. Tomorrow police, schools, the community!" one Berkeley Black Panther Party pamphlet celebrated. Yet organizing at the scale of the city could not constrain increasingly national and international capital.

BY THE LATE 1970s, the country had sunk into recession, experienced by capital as falling rates of profit and by workers as growing inflation and unemployment. Factories fled unionized cities for southern states and the global south, while automation made workers redundant. The scapegoat for ailing cities was not suburban and capital flight, which had drained public budgets, but the increasingly Black and Brown urban populations who relied on public services.[46] Welfare descended into fiscal and legitimacy crises. Riding a "law and order" backlash against sixties activism to power, the Nixon administration cemented a policy paradigm that conflated privatization and punishment. Both austerity and devolution, an offloading of responsibility from the federal government to lower jurisdictions, were political projects of disciplining the poor.[47]

Nixon's "silent majority" was based in the suburbs, where homeowners associations would become the institutional basis of a reactionary tax revolt.[48] In California, Howard Jarvis, then chief executive of the Apartment Association of Greater Los Angeles, led a statewide voter initiative to freeze property taxes in 1978; thereafter, houses would be taxed at 1 percent of their purchase price, and rates could only be increased by 2 percent a year.[49] Besides lavishing permanent benefits on the state's wealthiest homeowners, Proposition 13 more than halved California's budget, decimating its welfare, infrastructure, and public school spending.[50]

At the municipal level, debt proved a key bludgeon. With budgets constrained by austerity and taxes hollowed out by suburban flight, 1970s cities became more reliant on debt to stay afloat. Like individual homeowners, cities were disciplined by creditors and compelled to enact policies in line with business and real estate interests.[51] In New York, bondholders effected a hostile takeover of city governance, installing an unelected board to slash public spending and the wages of unionized, public sector workers— while they used the same workers' pension funds to backstop their plans.[52] Without the countervailing force of factory owners jockeying to keep land and property values down, and with capital on the hunt for more lucrative returns than could be had in productive industries, the stage was set for a transformation of cities into luxury playgrounds and luxury products.

BY THE EIGHTIES, shaped in turns by inflation, tax revolt, racism, and the red scare, Republicans had invented the housing programs that make up the overwhelming bulk of the government response to the housing question today, in which support for tenants ends up benefiting landlords and real estate developers. Through Nixon's Section 8 housing vouchers, the federal government covers the difference between market rent and a tenant's ability to pay. Reagan's convoluted Low Income Housing Tax Credit (LIHTC) subsidizes new development to purportedly produce affordable housing, privately owned apartments with only temporary rent caps, targeted predominantly at the middle class.[53] Thus, federal assistance for tenants came to subsidize the private market rather than regulate it, or offer a public alternative. As budgets drain, even tenants who qualify can't count on receiving aid, turning public assistance into a lottery. The programs help inflate the price of rent, eroding their usefulness: as rents rise, more tenants need support, while the state has to spend more money to house them. Rather than challenge the power of landlords and developers to extract rents, these programs hand over our tax dollars to shore up private profits.

Reagan made a sport of stripping support for the poor. In 1980, before he took office, the federal government provided resources that amounted to 22 percent of municipal budgets—resources that helped fund public housing as well as mass transit, hospitals and clinics, and other vital services from which entire regions benefited. By the end of Reagan's reign, that contribution had shrunk to 6 percent.[54] During this period, as part of an attack on all social welfare programs, the Housing and Urban Development budget was slashed by almost 80 percent. Public housing lost funding for even basic maintenance, and the administration installed a total ban on new public housing construction.[55] The HUD deputy assistant secretary insisted the government would be "getting out of the housing business. Period."[56] The results were as devastating as they were obvious: the homeless population of the country nearly doubled from 1984 to 1987.[57] In 1987, one review of LA's housing conditions found that 200,000 Latinx people were living in just 42,000 garages, most without plumbing, heat, or windows to the outside.[58]

The decline of public housing was timed with the expansion of another institution of publicly funded housing for the poor: prisons— public housing as public warehousing. Prisons capture predominantly poor and disproportionately Black and Brown tenants trapped in the vise of low wages, few jobs, and high rents. The US prison system has grown by a factor of six since the 1980s, a process that began after a decline in crime rates.[59] The explosive growth of incarceration mirrored rising municipal police budgets, which subjected residents of poor neighborhoods to increased harassment, surveillance, and arrest.[60] The effects were (and are) self-perpetuating. Criminalization produces categories of people ineligible for and "undeserving" of social support. Incarceration leaves people-sized chasms in kinship networks. Communities are disorganized by police, then policed for their disorganization.

Articulated in 1982 and implemented since the 1990s, "broken windows" is a theory of crime as contagion: lower-level offenses will bring higher ones. Like the horticultural metaphor of "urban blight" that figures dilapidation as disease, the theory smears the quality of tenants' neighborhoods into the character of tenants themselves. It suggests that buildings in poor condition are not evidence of historical segregation and disinvestment—the decisions of landowners and government—but evidence of residents' criminality.[61] The original architects of broken windows policing argued that police should produce not lower crime rates but rather "a sense of safety" and "public order" by eliminating from public space those people who signal its opposite, especially unhoused people.[62] The authors explicitly connect "order" to the local business climate.[63] Broken windows gave rise to a host of strategies that launder racial profiling as spatial profiling, including "hot spot" and "saturation policing," as well as area gang injunctions, which granted police so much discretionary power to stop, surveil, ticket, track, and jail that they were eventually declared illegal by the California Supreme Court.[64]

THE FUSION OF privatization and punishment was eagerly taken up as a mode of governance by Democrats in the Clinton era. The racialized connection between ownership and citizenship, lack of property and pathology, shaped which government expenses were understood as entitlements and which as welfare, as legitimate claims to public resources or as stigmatized handouts. The role of municipal governance continued to shift from providing services to existing residents to growing their economies and expanding their tax bases. Municipalities perform that role by courting new, richer residents as well as real estate speculators.[65] Besides a race to the bottom on tax claims, this "urban entrepreneurialism" promotes dumping public land and public assets into private hands and dismantling regulations to seduce investment. The privatization of public housing and elimination of local rent control regulations are both casualties of that effort.[66] Nearly 370,000 public

dwellings were destroyed under Clinton's HOPE VI program, a
bait-and-switch project that funded demolition of public housing
and its replacement by privately owned, publicly subsidized affordable housing.[67] And throughout the 1990s, thirty-two states passed
laws barring local jurisdictions from implementing or expanding
rent control.[68] The effects were measurable and visceral. When Boston repealed its rent stabilization laws in 1994, for example, both
median rent and the homeless population doubled.[69]

But profiteering from dwelling space would catch up to undermine even the stability of homeownership. Constant inflation
of property values exposed the lie at the heart of the American
dream. In 1999, Clinton tore down the legal boundaries between
banks and high-risk financial speculation, unleashing new financial
technologies that could be used to profit from housing. Enormous
financial actors, including real estate investment trusts (REITs)
like Invitation Homes and asset managers like Blackstone, sought
maximum returns by financializing a basic human need.[70] By 2007,
75 percent of US residential mortgage debt had been bundled
and sold in mortgage-backed securities.[71] In the collapse of 2008,
those securities went bust, and almost six million households lost
their homes to foreclosure or short sale, wiping out $2.5 trillion of
wealth, disproportionately from Black and Brown people.[72] Then,
Wall Street firms expanded their portfolios by capitalizing on the
crisis they had caused, pouring an estimated $60 billion into hous-
ing grabs.[73] Landlords and real estate speculators have crowded out
would-be homeowners from starting on the so-called property ladder, and twenty US cities have now shifted from a homeowner to a
tenant majority.[74]

DEVELOPER-IN-CHIEF DONALD TRUMP reflects both a new low and the same-old in real estate rule. His personal and family fortune was made by exploiting government land and housing policy. Trump's grandfather purchased land in Queens before the state paved roads, funded bridges, and subsidized the IRT subway there, all of which raised land values. His father, Fred Trump, profited from wartime housing incentives and the slum-clearance powers of the Federal Housing Act, all while refusing to rent to Black tenants in a systematic violation of fair housing. Donald Trump himself took advantage of giveaways of public land, blight designations, and fire-sale tax abatements to build luxury developments. He chased deregulation into the mortgage market, where he brokered $1 billion in predatory mortgages.[75]

As Trump's rise grotesquely demonstrates, the real estate industry has effectively captured state power; Sam Stein calls this amalgam "the real estate state."[76] While new financial pressures bear down on our homes, the ability to maximize returns is elevated by the state to a social good, privileged as the "best and highest use" of land and housing. While the state both abandons the poor to the private market and helps inflate the price of rent, more and more tenants find themselves living in poverty or occupying public space as a home. "In a good economy," LA's mayor Eric Garcetti would synthesize in 2020, "homelessness goes up."[77]

AFTER DECADES OF strategic abandonment, speculators have set their sights back on the city. Rich neighborhoods have seen waves of Disneyfication, and poor neighborhoods gentrification. Exploiting the false choice between urban decline and urban renewal, state actors collaborate with real estate speculators to channel capital into historically disinvested neighborhoods, inflating property values and rents. Eased by government incentives from Clinton's "empowerment zones" to Trump's "opportunity zones," global finance has migrated into precisely those neighborhoods where poor and working-class people had been stuck.

Just as the creation of the suburbs relied on collaboration between real estate and the state to create uneven, racialized space, so does contemporary gentrification—a "back to the city movement by capital," as geographer Neil Smith famously called it.[78] Gentrification does not revitalize urban neighborhoods, but eliminates poor and working-class people's material and symbolic ways of life. Like the widespread practice of arson in the 1970s, when landlords set abandoned buildings on fire to profit from insurance claims, the FIRE economy—the concatenation of finance, insurance, and real estate—must destroy in order to create. Displacement has ejected residents of color from cities and suburbanized poverty.[79] Today, for the first time, the majority of America's poor call the suburbs home.[80]

POLICE PLAY A central role in facilitating urban land grabs and inflating property values and rents. This is what Stop LAPD Spying Coalition calls "speculative policing."[81] As state policy continues to align with the profit motive, police act as the shock troops to make neighborhoods safer—not for residents but for speculative investment. Visible signs of poverty disrupt cities' capacities to court investors and sell themselves as products.[82] Thus, public resources are spent on harassing, ticketing, and incarcerating those who need housing, rather than housing them. From 2006 to 2019, the number of bans on camping, on sitting or lying in public, and on panhandling nearly doubled nationwide.[83]

Policing has helped fill the gap of legal segregation. Since the 1990s, "crime-free housing" ordinances have been used to exclude and evict mostly Black and Brown tenants in more than two thousand municipalities in forty-eight states.[84] The ordinances deputize white residents to police their neighbors of color, turning 3-1-1 and 9-1-1 calls into grounds for armed inspections, home raids, and banishment.[85]

Police also help facilitate the removal of people and the acquisition of housing for real estate gains. Nuisance laws allow police and city attorneys to target individual tenants by serving private landlords with demands to evict. In LA, tenants—predominantly poor, Black, and Brown tenants—are banished from blocks and entire neighborhoods, typically in newly gentrifying areas, based on testimony from police officers alone.[86]

In 2020, speculative policing resulted in the police execution of Breonna Taylor in Louisville, Kentucky. Taylor's ex-boyfriend, Jamarcus Glover, had rented a home at the center of a planned multimillion-dollar redevelopment initiative, for which Louisville officials had courted private investment with public subsidy. Deploying nuisance violations was part of the city's strategy for assembling the land for the project. Though capricious rules meant many properties qualified, the city concentrated nuisance filings around the redevelopment area, for as little as marijuana possession. In the three years preceding Taylor's killing, the city purchased twenty-eight properties on Glover's block, mostly through foreclosures initiated through nuisance claims, and demolished eight homes. In 2020, it used suspected drug offenses to issue a series of nuisance warnings to Glover's landlord. A "place-based investigation" identified Breonna Taylor as a "facilitator" of his activity and her house, ten miles away, as a "comfort site" that supported it. That tenuous link granted police the "no-knock" search warrant that allowed them to force their way into her apartment and kill her. Mission accomplished, the city purchased Glover's home for $1, on what would have been Taylor's twenty-seventh birthday.[87]

INSTITUTIONALIZING RACISM, ANTICOMMUNISM, and real estate greed, the state has chosen a side in the class war. Consider the two axes of current housing governance: individual homeownership on the one hand and mass incarceration on the other. Both should be considered publicly financed housing: one costs us $193 billion in subsidies; the other $182 billion in public debt and tax dollars.[88] But while one produces intergenerational wealth, the other erects barriers to employment and traps us in cycles of poverty and predation; while one christens upstanding "stakeholders" with full citizenship, the other brands the disenfranchised as "transients," deserving of punishment. And both cost at least three times what the government spends to support tenants.[89]

Promoting the private market as the solution to the social question of shelter has delegitimized the needs of poor and working-class, particularly Black and Brown, tenants and empowered landlords to draw profit from their continued immiseration. Rather than control rent with regulation or public competition, the state, under the thumb of the real estate industry, hands over tax dollars to landlords and developers. Trading public provision for private partnerships, regulations for market incentives, the US has pledged allegiance not to its citizens, but to property values and runaway rents.

Ending the One-Sided War

As tenants we live in the accumulated wreckage of this long war—the results of our occasional victories and more constant defeats. We tell this history from the vantage point of the real estate state because the war on tenants has been largely one-sided. Tenants have rarely mounted the organizational force to effectively combat its plots and designs. We experience that fallout not as a class, but in our individual biographies and the personal tragedies of our lives. History happens *to* us. But if we want to rewrite the next chapter of history with tenants as its subjects, we must confront these individual crises politically. Tenants cannot continue to be passive objects of social intervention but must be political agents, taking action in the context of our everyday lives. As LA Tenants Union cofounder Walt Senterfitt often reminds us, "It's not 'when we fight, we win,' but 'if we don't fight, we lose.'"

The word *comrade* entered the English language as the word for "roommate," naming those who lacked resources for privacy and came to share space—with strangers, friends, and lovers, all bound by the intimacy of having to pay rent.[90] But the shared proximity and vulnerability of tenancy—the exploitation and domination of rent—does not necessarily impel us to organize. We have to make an active effort. The rest of this book is devoted to that uphill battle. We describe concrete tenant struggles: direct, local conflicts that challenge the power of landlords and the real estate state. In so doing, these conflicts trace a future housing system governed not by individuated, asset-based welfare or repression and containment, but by collective self-determination and community control.

ON DECEMBER 3, 2023, nearly one thousand members of LATU took to the streets of Koreatown. Claiming the intersection of Vermont and Olympic, organizers played excerpts of the leaked LA City Council tape over a megaphone: the councilmembers' racist remarks about their own constituents and their scheme to gerrymander new districts to break up the power of tenants. Then councilmember Nury Martinez arrived—her likeness, anyway. Dressed in a wig and a skirt suit, the performer kissed the cheeks of another, playing a buttoned-up landlord, while he traveled around the intersection, demanding tenants pay up. Who should we look to for help to dismantle the real estate regime? What levers do we have? What threat do we pose? "What can we do today so that we can do tomorrow what we cannot do today?" in Paulo Freire's words. As our growing movement shows, to challenge the power of real estate at the scale of our buildings, cities, and beyond, tenants can look to each other. We can pick up the pieces in this wreckage and try to make this world our home.

CHAPTER 3

THE RETURN
OF THE RENT STRIKE

"Rights are what you make and what you take."
–James Boggs

WE'VE HEARD THE story quite a few times over the course of our organizing. It's a tenant's first night on rent strike, and what they're shocked by most of all is that nothing, really, occurs. The building doesn't crumble around them. Their keys still open the locks. The roof remains above their heads. Their home, though they have not paid for it, persists. Their surprise is telling. Every night before this one, their ability to have shelter depended on a payment to their landlord—that monthly tribute we call rent. We often hear of the lengths to which our union's members will go to ensure that this payment is made: they will forgo food, medication, or basic necessities; secure a pay-day loan or borrow from individuals at extortionate interest; pawn their tools, instruments, valuables; pick up extra shifts, or even second and third jobs. Many of our members have already experienced eviction, have doubled up with family, stayed in cars, or pitched tents in public space. Rent is a constant burden and fear, one that installs itself in the places we live, one that makes the consequences of not paying feel as dramatic as a building's collapse. Sometimes, it's only after tenants decide to withhold rent on purpose that the absurdity of rent becomes clear.

PERHAPS NO OTHER experience can provide us with the same insight into the parasitic role of landlords and the power of collective action than withholding rent in coordination with our neighbors. Rent strikes lay claim to housing as a human right—to shelter, no matter tenants' ability or willingness to pay for it. Yes, this claim is temporary: the rent strikes we've organized have lasted only as long as a few years. Yes, it's risky: victory isn't guaranteed. But it's powerful: rent strikes stop the flow of cash to our landlords and reveal *their* dependence on *us*. Rent strikes suggest that the right to housing already exists; all we need to do is claim it.

For an individual building, a rent strike is a crucial tactic of tenant militancy, a weapon with the power to push back against everyday exploitation and win tenants' demands. It can create enough leverage for poor and working-class tenants to force rich and well-connected landlords to heel. This leverage can be exercised without recourse to government representatives or city officials and without changes in the law. Our building-wide strikes have earned tenants rent cancellations, rent reductions, direct payments, structural repairs, the restoration of amenities, and more.

Of course, we know the struggle for a just housing system isn't won when a single landlord backs down. A single rent strike will not abolish rent. Yet rent strikes, besides extracting concessions, build lasting organizations for poor and working-class people to fight back against the exploitation and domination of rent long-term. Each rent strike builds new competencies, from collective decision-making, to escalation tactics, to negotiation techniques. Each rent strike produces long-term relationships, shaped by the experience of collective struggle. Each rent strike both tests and builds our capacity. Each rent strike develops the power of tenants as political subjects. A bridge between the utopian future we want and the practical capacities we need to get there, each rent strike is a step forward in realizing the seemingly impossible—a world without landlords, a world without rent.

Though withholding rent has put their housing in jeopardy, tenants on rent strike often feel a stronger sense of ownership over that housing than they've ever felt before. Rent strikes are a means and guide us toward the ends of our work. One way to envision rent abolition is as an extension of a rent strike. Our task is to grow the power of our movement enough to make rent strikes general and—finally—permanent. This would demand a phase of struggle that has yet to come: a coordinated rent strike not isolated in one building, but across a city, even nationwide. This is the kind of power we would need to begin to transform property relations as well as the state that guarantees them. By proliferating and uniting individual building struggles, we pave the road to rent abolition together.

IN THIS CHAPTER, we focus on a single, successful rent strike, carried out by Los Mariachis de Union de Vecinos of Boyle Heights. The almost yearlong rent strike, supported by the LA Tenants Union, resulted in a collective bargaining agreement that lowered rents, guaranteed repairs, and secured the right to renegotiate. We show how we did it and how anyone can repeat it, what conditions it made possible in that building, and what space it opened for tenants everywhere. We draw on the reflections of tenants in the Union de Vecinos association, as well as those of the LA Tenants Union organizers who supported them throughout, to describe the struggle in their own words.

It is tempting to view the Mariachi struggle as a unique, unrepeatable case—as unprecedented as it is unlikely. A building of working-class immigrants, some undocumented, were willing to risk eviction from their long-term homes, the scarlet letter of an eviction record, their energy and precious time. But we hope this chapter demonstrates just how ordinary the steps they took to this victory were—how they found, in their daily life and in their building, ways to build trust with each other, to create and execute a strategy, and to win the right to stay put. Their action did not happen in a vacuum; the tenants were not alone. They relied on the support of their community, lawyers willing to listen and support the tenants' own plans, and their citywide tenants union.

Los Mariachis' year of effort was built around one simple, purposeful *in*action: the building-wide withholding of rent. It reflects a common response to a tenant's first experience of injustice: in the face of a rent increase, a leak, or landlord harassment, we're overwhelmed by the instinct to revolt, react, and simply not pay rent. What are we paying for, anyway? Why should we have to pay at all? This righteous anger, the will to refuse, usually stomped out by necessity and habit, is as present as our fear.

Aquí queremos vivir:
Los Mariachis de Union de Vecinos

In January 2017, Alejandro Juárez received a notice announcing that his new landlord would be raising his rent from $840 to $1,495—a $655 increase. A construction worker and Mexican immigrant, Juárez had lived in his beige stucco building on Second Street, just one block away from Mariachi Plaza, for more than ten years. The rent increase, he discovered, was legal. The twenty-four apartments in his building were not subject to rent stabilization, and no other laws stood in the way of the routine profiteering that drives long-term residents from their long-term homes. By law, the building's owner was entitled to charge whatever the market—not the current tenants—could bear.

Residents of Boyle Heights have fought state-sanctioned displacement in every decade of the neighborhood's history. They fought against the Mexican repatriation campaigns of the 1930s; against the forced internment of Japanese immigrants in the 1940s; against the urban renewal projects of the 1960s, when freeway construction displaced ten thousand residents and took over more than 12 percent of neighborhood land.[1] In the 1990s, public housing tenants organized against Clinton's HOPE VI "revitalization" program, which demolished their homes and displaced over one thousand families.[2] In the 2000s, residents began to fight gentrification—a displacement project as much produced by government policy as those from decades before.[3] Relying on tax incentives, rezonings, LA Metro's expansion, and ballooning LAPD patrols, real estate speculators had converged on Boyle Heights—they'd even lobbied to launder bonuses through an Arts District designation. Over twenty years, property values tripled and median rents doubled, pushing out poor and working-class tenants who had called Boyle

Heights home for their whole lives.[4] In their gentrifying neighborhood, where the powers of policy and policing underwrite developer greed, the Second Street tenants had a target on their backs.

In the building's hallways and parking lot, next to its trash cans,
out on the street, Alejandro Juárez asked his neighbors if they'd
received rent increase notices. A few had. More worried they'd be
next. Juárez had heard about the LA Tenants Union from a family member and asked his neighbors to join him at the next meeting of its Eastside chapter.[5] At that first meeting, Juárez felt a mix
of relief and fury in telling his story and discovering his building
was not alone. Tenants across the neighborhood were under attack.
Just blocks away, he learned, a nonprofit developer called the East
Los Angeles Community Corporation (ELACC) had purchased a
rent-stabilized building, then announced plans to demolish it and
redevelop the site. The company said current tenants could join the
public lottery for a few spots in affordable housing, but even those
who got those spots wouldn't be able to afford their rents.[6] But the
tenants had organized, campaigned to undermine ELACC's legitimacy and challenge its nonprofit status, and won twenty households the right of return.

This story was not unique: that same year, Juárez learned, the
Hollins Tenants Association had been targeted for removal by a
landlord who'd named "white artists" as his desired tenants, but they
also fought back and protected twenty homes. And the twenty-eight
households of the Michigan Heights Tenants Association had suc-
cessfully fought for eight months against 40 percent rent increases—
in a non-rent-stabilized building like Juárez's own. Refusing to pay
the increases and submitting only their original rent, they forced
their landlord to the bargaining table and won a two-year contract
for guaranteed repairs and rents they could afford. In each case, ten-

ants organizing with the union had been able to temper the despotic control of landlords and developers over their neighborhood and claim some measure for themselves.

LATU organizer Elizabeth Blaney invited Juárez to host a building meeting in the Eastside Local's Union de Vecinos office that week. He wasn't sure what to expect when he made the invitation. As his neighbor Isabel (Isa) Ramirez, a food service and domestic worker, said later, the tenants didn't know a thing about each other before the meeting, "not even each other's names."[7] But seventeen tenants turned out. Most of them had lived in the building for over a decade and could see the ring tightening around Boyle Heights; land and business owners were squeezing out the infrastructure residents relied on. A luxury development had replaced homes where they'd gathered with friends. New restaurants had opened with menus written only in English. Laundromats had been shuttered and galleries opened in their place.

The tenants introduced themselves and began to take stock. That fall, they'd all received word that their building would be changing hands. Just after New Year's in 2017, seven out of the twenty-four apartments had received official notices that rents would be going up. Before they could organize, they had to realize they weren't alone. The tenants opened up about the building's role in their lives. Melissa (Meli) Reyes wanted stability for her aging mother Gloria and to see her younger brother finish school undisturbed. Actor Francisco Gonzalez relied on his proximity to the Metro Gold Line to commute to auditions. Brothers Luis and Enrique Valdivia, whose rent increase was the highest in the group, at $800 a month, had shared an apartment in the building for more than twenty years. The Valdivias, like a full third of the building's residents, were mariachi musicians, who relied on Mariachi

Plaza to pick up work, an almost century-long tradition that gave the plaza its name. For the mariachis, to lose their home would also mean to lose their livelihood. At the end of the meeting, the tenants went around in a circle, one by one. Would they commit to organizing together? Would they fight to stay in their homes? Every tenant said yes.

A Craigslist ad for an apartment in their building animated their commitment to each other. The "affordable luxury apartment" in the listing's photos was renovated with distressed-wood floors and pristine white walls and staged with mid-century-modern furniture. Figuring Boyle Heights as a place to leave rather than a place to live, the ad called the neighborhood "an ideal location for commuters . . . minutes from Downtown." It even rebranded the building with a new name: "Mariachi Crossing." The new landlord, Melissa Reyes put it later, was "trying to make money under the name of the mariachis, at the same time he was displacing mariachis," leveraging the neighborhood's past to erase its present.[8] Taking on both the community's iconography and the position of the most vulnerable members of their association, the tenants began referring to themselves as Los Mariachis de Union de Vecinos. The people who gave the neighborhood its culture would not willingly be displaced.

Together, the group decided on their first collective action: they wanted a meeting with the property manager. In the notices they'd received, the landlord tied rent increases to necessary maintenance, but he'd made only superficial changes. He'd installed a fence with horizontal slats—an aesthetic so predictable we call them "gentrification fences"—and put out potted succulents. He hadn't made any repairs inside their homes. The tenants each cataloged the violations in their apartments, filling out the union's inspection form: water damage from leaks, suspicious mold, termite-bitten doorways, filthy vents. They collected the forms into a dossier and delivered them to the property manager by hand. For two weeks, they prepped for the meeting. But when it finally happened, they left dazed and discouraged. About the tenants' need for repairs, the manager was evasive, but about the rent increases he was clear: there was nothing he would do.

The new landlord wanted to use raised rents to cover his purchase price—his speculative investment—not better living conditions and hid his identity under an LLC. No one even knew his real name, yet he had the power to determine who could and could not continue to live in homes they'd lived in for decades. Members of the LATU Local understood the assignment: track down his identity. They searched public records, Google, and Facebook across a chain of LLCs. They collected a list of physical addresses and paid each one an in-person visit. Even Blaney's daughter got involved; for a few days, she posed as if selling chocolates door-to-door. Finally, they connected the building to its owner, Frank "BJ" Turner. Putting a face and a name on the landlord turned the struggle against an impersonal process of gentrification into a struggle against a would-be evictor, who could no longer hide from personal responsibility for—and personal benefit from—the tenants' removal.

A solicitation deck for Dunleer Investments, founded by Turner, confirmed they'd found their target.[9] It listed key features of their building to entice investors: it was "non-rent controlled" (a phrase both underlined and italicized), in a neighborhood "slated for new 'metro-centric' development," and had a projected rate of return of 20 percent. The deck promised potential clients access to a "rapidly gentrifying" submarket—a self-fulfilling prophecy of speculation—and identified not just asking rents for the property, but kinds of renters: "millennial tenants . . . [who were] willing to pay" for good design in "jeans and coffee." For those tenants, it insisted, "housing is less of a financial decision, more of a lifestyle decision." For the current tenants, the document was evidence that they stood in between the new owner and his plans: displacement and replacement for profit.

In February 2017, the tenants sent Turner a letter under LATU's letterhead, announcing that they'd formed an association and had the support of a union. The first demand was a modest one: they wanted to meet face-to-face. They wanted to discuss needed repairs, the behavior of the onsite manager, and to "negotiate a more just increase," as Luis Valdivia put it at the time—one that allowed them to keep their homes and matched the scale of investment they saw in bettering their living conditions. "The owner wants to wash his hands of us now that he changed out the stove and put in a new AC," Luis Valdivia told *LA Weekly*, "The only option we have is to struggle to keep what we have and try to negotiate."[10] At first, Turner simply ignored their request.

The association responded to his silence by getting louder. They decorated their building with posters and collages, papering over the facade. "20 years living here 80% rent hike," read one; "$800 más por mes es irrazonable"' read another. One sign pictured a cartoon of a smiling, blond-haired Turner kicking three mariachi musicians to the curb. They hung the LATU banner across the parking lot: "Where will you go when you can't afford your neighborhood? Why not fight to stay?" Making the art helped build relationships for an afternoon; living with that art re-signified their homes as sites of political struggle. The art became "part of where I live, and where I continue to live," Ramirez said.[11]

On April 1, the group held a press conference and celebration in Mariachi Plaza, calling on the community for support. In a gesture that would become a signature throughout their struggle, the resident musicians dressed in mariachi regalia—embroidered suits and matching sombreros—and played music for the crowd. Their next action was more aggressive: the Mariachis played at the property manager's office.

Had the tenants turned to most available resources—the helpline at LA's housing department, elected officials' constituent services, or LA's few, overburdened legal aid efforts—they likely would have been told nothing could be done. Established legal services respond to conflict between landlords and tenants as casework for individual clients, the outcome of which is prescribed in advance by current tenant law. Lacking capacity to support a lengthy process with uncertain ends, most nonprofit organizations treat collective action as a liability to be avoided rather than a road to victory. For government representatives, the Mariachi tenants could serve as an example of why laws might need to be changed. They could be pointed to as symbolic leverage for a long legislative process, in order to benefit others in the future after they'd tragically but inevitably lost their homes. In the procedural arenas of the courts and elections, tenants are helped only after harm has occurred. They are victims, passive objects of political intervention, rather than political agents themselves.

"EVERYTHING IS LEGAL," Francisco Gonzalez told *Marketplace* about his and the group's perspective at first. "This is gonna be the new norm, and that's it."[12] The insufficiency of tenants' legal protections is often presented as a reality we have no choice but to accept, as if legal rights dictate the sum total of what's possible to achieve. Under current law, tenants' rights are framed in the negative, as carve-outs that establish the limits of what landlords can do, infringements on a landlord's property rights, not protections for preserving a tenant's human need.

But as they continued to meet, the Mariachi tenants came to understand rights not as upper limits but as instruments. "Tenants' rights" became ingredients in the organizing adage of "turning what you have into what you need to get what you want." The association learned about California's protections for undocumented people, which prevent landlords from turning over information on immigration status. "I learned that even though I don't have papers, I have rights," one member of the association said. They learned about the First Amendment right to organize and California's statutes against retaliation for organizing, which make tenants associations not only legal, but a strategic form of protection in court. They learned about the warranty of habitability, implied in most every state and enshrined in California, which ties a tenant's obligation to pay rent to a property's livability: an apartment free of pests and structural issues, heat that heats, lights that light, drains that drain. Withholding rent is often legally protected if basic living standards are not met.

They also realized that they would have to take on the fight themselves. "Almost always, people are more ready to take risks than many nonprofits think they are," Elizabeth Blaney later told *KnockLA*. As organizers, "our job is to bring people together, to look at the different options out there and the different paths, to bring information about risks and how we can take risks together, and to encourage people around what is possible."[13] Certainly, the law affirmed the landlord's right to force the long-term tenants from their homes. The Mariachi tenants chose to fight not for what was legal, but for what was *right*.

What if they withheld rent? Blaney had raised the idea of a rent strike before, but the association had wanted to wait. They tried communicating with the landlord. They tried protest. They even submitted a letter from the councilmember representing their district, who encouraged the landlord to negotiate. But since none of those things got the landlord's attention, maybe an impact on his pocketbook would. Sure, they could lose their housing. But for many of the tenants who'd received rent increases, those notices were no different from evictions, anyway. If they paid just their original rent, they'd already be at risk. For those tenants, the decision was clear. On June 1, 2017, they stopped paying rent. "At this point," Gonzalez said, "there's nothing else we can lose."[14]

THE STRIKE HAS long been a weapon of the poor and the working class. Just as withholding labor upends the power relation between worker and boss, withholding rent upends the power relation between tenant and landlord. Strikes reverse and reveal relations of dependence: rather than the worker depending on the boss for a wage, the boss depends on the worker to produce profit; rather than the tenant depending on the landlord for housing, the landlord depends on the tenant to extract rent. Strikes are not symbolic actions. Issuing a "negative sanction," to use Frances Fox Piven and Richard A. Cloward's phrase, strikes do not express a demand; they force concessions.[15] They reassert the power of poor and working-class people to shape the terms of their lives—in short, their power to make and break history.

The rent strike has been a tactic of tenant militancy for more than a century. In the Great Rent Wars of the early 1900s, ten thousand Jewish immigrants housed in the dank tenements of New York's Lower East Side organized with the Tenants Defense Union. They withheld rent from slumlords and battled police to block evictions. Their efforts secured the county's first housing regulations and the first rent controls—major and enduring working-class victories.[16] In the mid-1960s, when slum conditions and segregation were symbolized in a swelling infestation of rats, more than five hundred buildings across Harlem joined a rent strike supported by the Congress of Racial Equality. They won rent reductions, tenant protections, and public funds for extermination and repairs.[17]

As we see in how our landlords treat us and neglect our apartments, the laws that govern evictions, leases, and building codes are only as good as they are enforced—mostly, they're ignored. Rent strikes can act as collective enforcement for rights we have and even win us those we don't. But rent strikes have fallen out of our arsenal, suppressed by the red scare, diffused by working-class disorganization, and discouraged by the professionalization of expected agents of social change. To revive the rent strike demands that we reorder our beliefs about what is possible and who can bring it about. It is to take a leap of faith grounded in a sense of political agency: that tenants themselves can be, must be, the ones to fight for ourselves.

The mariachi tenants who received rent increases had begun to withhold their rent. But what if all the tenants in the building did? It would take more than twice the number of individual eviction cases to get rid of them. In the meantime, the landlord would lose more than twice the rent. But would other tenants be willing to take the same risk? Though they shared a landlord, not every tenant shared the same willingness to fight; not every tenant was a musician for whom the loss of home was bound to loss of work; not every tenant was under extreme economic pressure to resist a rent increase. Many feared retaliation from police and ICE. A few believed displacement was inevitable, that they should accept the situation because there was nothing they could do.

The strikers set to work expanding their numbers. They addressed concerns with accurate information: You can't be tossed out of your home without an order from the court. A posted notice may feel like the end of the world, but it isn't final; landlords often depend on lack of understanding to intimidate you out of your home. Eviction is a process, one that requires the landlord's time and money, and one that tenants can stretch and bend as best they can. There will be filing errors. You can request a jury trial and slow things down. And the whole time during that process, there are many points at which to settle the case or leave without a black mark. The first wave of rent strikers were already modeling these truths. Cops hadn't arrived. Their belongings remained inside. They continued to wake up every morning in the apartments they were fighting for.

A few tenants had reservations about "making trouble," as Ramirez characterized one of her own fears. She had always considered it a virtue to be polite, and engaging in direct confrontation with her landlord felt like a betrayal of her values. But conflict, the group reminded each other, had been the one to knock on their door. Another doubt was assuaged by hearing about the strategy of a rent strike from their peers. Was it more than a theory or a hypothetical, something people could actually do? Representatives from the Michigan Tenants Association made a trip to their building to share the details of their struggle. The tenants heard the idea of a rent strike not just from organizers who said it could work, but from tenants like them for whom it already had.

After a month of group meetings, one-on-ones, potlucks, and bake sales, the association doubled the number of strike participants. For the strikers who hadn't received increases, participation was based on both solidarity and self-interest, and the promise of concert between the two. "In solidarity with the others, we said they're coming for us next, and we stood with our neighbors," as Jose Sanchez, one of the solidarity strikers, told *LA Taco*.[18] At the end of June, the association held a meeting and went around one by one in a circle again. Would you withhold your rent? Would you join the strike? Fifteen said yes. The group generated a set of agreements about what it meant to be part of the strike: they would keep their rent, refuse to accept individual deals, decline to get individual lawyers, and commit to sharing doubts with the group before making a decision alone. Every tenant signed. July 1, 2017, was the first night of the wider collective strike. The building didn't fall.

A RENT STRIKE both exercises and builds power, using the two central tools tenants have at their disposal: solidarity and rent checks. One tenant's inability to pay is not a strike. What makes a rent strike a *strike* is consciousness and coordination. This is clear from the Mariachis' collective action: Those who couldn't pay and those who could decided to join together, organizing to withhold a majority of the rent roll for the building. The association turned withholding rent into a ritual, turning over their rent checks or money orders to be stored by the union each month. Collecting the checks helped visualize the money they held as leverage, measured individual accountability, and asserted their commitment to the strike. Knowing unity was essential, the association made decisions by consensus. "In itself, we haven't had a leader within the group," Ramirez explained. "All of us are one group, all of us have to give our opinion, and what we think. All of us say, all of us vote, all of us decide."[19] Their economic leverage would have been impossible without the relationships they built as equal participants in their association—and as neighbors.

Underneath political agency there is communal life. The association met every Thursday, sharing reservations as well as excitement—and a lot of food. Ramirez talked about the ritual of going to meetings and marches, which shaped her time and her understanding of her housing. At first she thought, "He's a millionaire. He can kick us out. He's gonna have the better lawyers. He's got money." Then she would remember, "We're a group, and if we continue supporting each other, we're going to go forward."[20] The strength of her association was manifest not only in its ability to assert demands, but in its power to create relationships of trust, mutual aid, care, and support. Ramirez didn't remember signing the strike agreement; she remembered feeling comfortable enough to ask to borrow an onion from her neighbor.

The Mariachi strike became more than a struggle for one building, but for the soul of the neighborhood. "Of course we were afraid," Sanchez summarized. "Because we don't know. Nobody can guarantee you that you're going to win this battle ... Sometimes you want to go to sleep and you feel like, 'Jeez, am I doing the right thing? Why did I have to do this? Maybe I should look for another place?' ... But where? Everywhere is expensive ... Why should I have to be kicked out of this place? You know? This is my home. This is where I've lived for so many years."[21]

Drawing on members of the Union de Vecinos local chapter and the LA Tenants Union, Los Mariachis built on the expertise of tenants in their own communities, who'd used collective power to protect themselves against displacement, pushing those strategies further. Indeed, the LA Tenants Union helped create the context and conditions that made the strike thinkable in the first place, sustainable in the near term, and possible to win. Los Mariachis relied on the support of their union siblings to share their stories, to donate to their fundraisers, to participate in their campaign, to show up to protests and make their actions a success. Even Ramirez's four-year-old niece would ask to join her at the actions, chanting "¡Boyle Heights No Se Vende!" in the crowd.

The landlord responded to their show of solidarity by offering individual deals. Irma Aguilar was offered two months' free rent and $2,000 cash to leave. The tenants held a meeting to think through the offers. To some, the offers they'd received sounded like windfalls. But when they calculated moving costs and looked at rents elsewhere, they realized accepting the money would mean relocating not to another apartment in the neighborhood but to another city or even another state. "It's a strategy," Irma Aguilar told *LA Weekly*. "The owner wants to peel us off in small groups over time, rather than all at once."[22] They could proceed as individuals to an end known in advance, or they could stick together and see what else there was to gain.

But for the organizing to work, the tenants had to hold off their landlord in court. The eviction process had begun. Blaney stressed that attorneys Tyler Anderson and Noah Greenberg of Los Angeles Center for Community Law and Action "very clearly understood their role. That they were not here to direct our strategy, or to win the case and save the people. . . . They understood that the rent strike was an organizing strategy, and the legal strategy was to give that organizing strategy more time."[23] To stall court appearances, note every filing error, request every continuance and a jury for each trial, was to allow the strike to build pressure, both politically, as support for their cause grew, and economically, as each month compounded the impact on the landlord's bottom line. Preventing the landlord from being able to resolve the issue through the courts meant he'd have to face off with the tenants themselves.

Seizing the campaign to secure their own housing put the tenants in control of the physical space of their building as well. In July 2017, two members of the association, a couple who had signed on to the strike as solidarity strikers, were awarded an apartment from a city lottery: an extremely rare chance for steeply subsidized housing, with rents at $400. Given Karen's health, the rent would mean more resources for her care. They called an emergency meeting in their apartment and the group made a collective decision. Rather than hand the keys over to their landlord and weaken the strike, they would give them to the association—and continue to assume the economic responsibility of the strike. The association turned the vacant apartment into a common space, used for meetings, art making, shared meals, and parties. Taking over the apartment demonstrated a key aspect of their fight: a rent strike is an occupation by another name—a temporary claim of the housing we live in as the housing we need and deserve.

In June, the landlord had agreed to meet with tenants, but only as individuals, and not at their apartment building, but at an undisclosed hotel. He also demanded the tenants submit to security checks and bring IDs. For the Latinx tenants, some of whom were undocumented, "the conditions were racist," Elizabeth Blaney said.[24] The association refused the meetings, recognizing the request as a tactic to pit tenants against each other and lure them out one by one. The property management company continued their own pressure campaign: ignoring maintenance requests and enforcing strict rules around guests and parking spaces.

The tenants didn't merely refuse to pay rent and wait for the landlord to come to his senses. They relied on social and political pressure as well. Beyond the economic sanction of the strike, they staged a series of escalations to constrain his decision. Regular, disruptive

protests made them a fixture in the neighborhood, where the iden-
tification with mariachis, a beloved Boyle Heights "icon," as Blaney
recalled, became "a hook to build public support."[25] Those actions
also won them relentless coverage in mainstream media, multiple
features in the usually unsympathetic *LA Times*, and regular appearances on local news.[26] "We wanted to make sure that the owner, every
time he watched TV and turned on the news, we are the news," Francisco Gonzalez summarized.[27]

THE LANDLORD'S CONTINUED intransigence inspired direct
confrontation. By late summer, the association stepped up their
offense. They coordinated an online action to flood the landlord's
social media with comments; Turner deleted his accounts. Then
they organized a protest in front of the landlord's home in Rancho Park, fourteen miles away from their own neighborhood. The
distance made literal the relationship of dependency of rich neighborhoods on poor ones, the wealth extracted from the city that
circulates in the suburbs. "We needed to go to his neighborhood,
to his house, to bring the fight to his front door," Blaney said. "In
eleven months he didn't want to show his face. He didn't want to
talk to the tenants that he was trying to force out."[28] LLCs offer
landlords anonymity and a shield from accountability beyond
a geographic divide. The apparatus of the courts helps establish
polite distance between the dirty work of eviction and a landlord's
private life. But eviction is personal for us; it should be personal for
our landlords, too.

On a weeknight in September 2017, the tenants and almost a
hundred supporters gathered in front of the landlord's front door.
They chanted "Housing is a human right, not just for the rich and

white," talked about their connection to their own homes, and enjoyed spiced hot cocoa and pan dulce a few of the residents had brought to share. They knocked on doors surrounding Turner's building, handed out flyers—"Do you know your neighbor is a slumlord?"—and explained why they were there. Some of Turner's neighbors complained about the disruption. One crumpled the flier he'd been handed and threw it back at the group. Are these long-term tenants "less deserving of a home, so that BJ can put his ideal tenant in there?" Blaney called through a bullhorn. Turner's curtains remained drawn and the door remained closed.

THE TENANTS AND organizers understood the protests at the landlord's house as the final impetus for him to agree to negotiate. "When the shoe was on the other foot, and the harassment started going in the opposite direction, that is what made him give in," Sanchez said.[29] Ramirez echoed the effectiveness of "shaming," imagining that his wife and his neighbors had pressured him to come to the bargaining table. The landlord agreed to sit down with the group as a whole—if the tenants would call off another planned demonstration at his home.

Arriving at the bargaining table that first day, the tenants had already transformed the balance of power. They'd stalled the landlord in court. They'd shamed him at his front door. They'd won the symbolic support of their council representative and the press. They'd gathered hundreds of their neighbors into their fight. And they'd deprived Turner of almost a year of rent. Before bargaining began that day, every tenant got to speak, to introduce themselves and tell their story. "So they could say, I'm a human being," Blaney said, "I am a person that exists here."[30]

The group turned to forming consensus on the terms of an agreement they would accept. That process reflected the internal culture of tenant democracy built throughout the strike. Lawyers on either side traded proposals and counterproposals for the bargaining agreements—removing a gag order and limitations on future protest were key sticking points.

Unsatisfied with their landlord's offers, the tenants returned to Rancho Park in December 2017. That action made a direct connection between the displacement of poor and working-class tenants and the rise of homelessness in LA. As night fell, protesters from LATU and DSA-LA set up a small group of tents on a strip of sidewalk just beyond Turner's home. "Tomorrow we might be homeless because of BJ Turner" the signs affixed to their temporary encampment read. Four police officers in two SUVs arrived on site, yet because protestors were on public property, a confrontation did not stop the action. Running the law against its grain, the group relied on a legal settlement that had forced the city to allow unhoused tenants to leave their tents up overnight. The group slept and rose on the sidewalk in front of Turner's home.

The trial for the eviction of Gloria Reyes, Melissa's mom, was the first court date set. But jury selection never occurred. On February 12, 2018, after more than a year of struggle, the tenants and the landlord signed a collective bargaining agreement—the first of its kind in LA history. The agreement canceled six months of withheld rent, brought the original average increase down to under a quarter of the landlord's original demand, capped yearly future increases at 5 percent, and included a guarantee that the landlord would make all requested repairs or was not entitled to collect rent. The contract recognized the tenants' right to form an association and to bargain collectively for this and each subsequent lease. Through a yearlong rent strike, direct actions that brought the struggle to where their landlord lived, and broad community support, the tenants won an equivalent of rent control for their building, an enforcement mechanism for maintenance, and the right to negotiate their contract collectively thereafter.

"TODAY, GENTRIFICATION IS not inevitable," Blaney announced at the celebration, where tenants ate, danced, and mariachis played. "It feels glorified," Francisco Gonzalez said. "By being organized, by working together, you can get some power."[31] When she first saw the rent increase notice, Reyes explained, the risks of losing their home seemed more familiar than the risks of fighting for it. She recalled the fear but also the thrill of experimentation that had characterized their fight. "We felt like we were making it up at some level. Sometimes we didn't know if the things we were doing were gonna generate something. There were no guarantees."[32] Practiced in facing the unknown together, Los Mariachis began a second strike when the pandemic hit. Bolstered by LATU's citywide "Food Not Rent" campaign and protected by a moratorium on evictions, they maintained that strike for nearly three years.

Rent strikes are acts of collective defiance: both in behavior and belief. They are economic, political, and cultural interventions: they can preserve housing for poor and working-class tenants, produce lasting democratic infrastructures based on relationships of shared risk and solidarity, and foster a celebratory culture of resistance. They suspend the normal course of exploitation and make further action possible.

In their fight, Los Mariachis affirmed their role as producers of the value of Boyle Heights and their right to share in that value. Relying on legal support to stall their evictions rather than win their case, refusing to abide by the laws that failed to protect their homes, Los Mariachis believed in their own capacity to interrupt the naturalized course of displacement and erect a barrier to the tide of gentrification. By withholding rent as a tenants association, they transformed individual inability to pay into collective leverage. They used their own power—tenant power—and their own resources to change their conditions themselves. But just as they relied on the tenant movement for inspiration and support, the mariachis' victory is the victory of the community, the neighborhood, the local chapter, the union, and tenants everywhere.

CHAPTER 4

LA LUCHA EDUCA

"It takes courage to say that the good were defeated not because
they were good, but because they were weak."
—Bertolt Brecht

THE FIRST LA Tenants Union meeting was a "renter's rights work-shop." Soon, we realized, all three parts of that framework had to go. "Renter," because we had to broaden our understanding of the populations who live in antagonism to rent, including people who live outside. "Workshop," because we couldn't just offer resources to individual tenants and send them on their way. "Rights," because what few tenants had weren't easy to use and didn't stop landlords from acting otherwise. And the right we want to win, the human right to housing, will take another kind of housing system, another kind of state, and another kind of world. The tenants union is the vehicle to move toward that world *now*. If tenants want to change our material conditions we have to change the power relations that keep those conditions in place. We need power ourselves.

How could we build a world in which tenants could claim hous-ing as a right? We're often told that politics begins and ends with legislation. Politics is what happens in city council, in the state capitol, or in the White House. In this dominant view, politics is synonymous with policy. To intervene in power relations between us and our landlords, we're told that we should leverage their mediator, the state. We should express our preferences with our votes, naming people to represent our interests in the halls of government, where policy is made. Between elections, we should gather constituencies to pressure those individuals. In this view, the state—not our landlords—should be the object of our collective justice work.

But policy is not a neutral tool that balances the interests of tenants and landlords. Policy reflects and congeals class power; it is a tool for class war. The founding document of the United States, the Constitution, designed our electoral process around protecting property holders from the propertyless. US housing policy has privileged homeowners over tenants, and private, asset-based wealth over a social wage. Even programs aimed at supporting the poor prioritize privately owned, publicly subsidized housing: they entail payments to landlords or developers to prop up their profits and help them hoard land. The history of housing policy is a war on tenants, a love affair between the state and real estate.

We don't need the annual scandal of politicians accepting real estate bribes to see the influence of the industry on our laws. Our rent checks fund the real estate lobby that organizes against us. The National Association of Realtors claim a top spot among spenders on federal lobbying each year. The California Association of Realtors is the second-largest donor to the state's Democratic Party. Landlord "stakeholders" claim their property taxes are *their* contributions to the public good, but it is we who pay our landlords' property taxes. Despite a demographic majority in many cities, tenants make up a tiny minority of elected officials, representatives,

and judges. In the California state legislature, out of 120 representatives, only 5 are tenants, and more than a fourth are landlords.[1]
Undocumented tenants have even less power, barred from deciding
the laws that govern their lives. Unhoused tenants face immense
barriers to civic participation; to register to vote demands a permanent address. Some incarcerated and formerly incarcerated tenants
are denied the franchise altogether.

When tenants win rights enshrined by legislation, it's because
we've fought our landlords. The mass rent strikes in New York's
Lower East Side tenements brought us building codes that mandate basic habitability standards, the requirement of a court process to legally evict, and the country's first rent controls.[2] During
World War II, militant tenants physically blocked evictions and
inspired national protections against price gouging in the form of
rent control. The tenant movement of the 1960s and '70s, including an intrepid squatters movement that laid claim to abandoned
housing, managed to reestablish limits that had been rolled back
in cities nationwide.[3] Like all history, housing policy is a product of
class struggle.

But decades-long efforts to disorganize tenants and the working
class as a whole have removed collective struggle from our arsenal.
Capitalists have decimated labor unions, eroded working-class institutions, and enclosed public space. As reform replaced confrontation
as the sole avenue for change, power to effect policy has been hoarded
among professional experts and elites. In housing, economists and
urban planners gained prominence as policy guides, speaking not
on our behalf but over us.[4] Their methodological biases (homes are
interchangeable "units"; regulation is "government interference")
as well as money-laundered research (from think tanks funded by
real estate firms) are smeared into their so-called objectivity. Even

scholarship that details the racial disparities of eviction or the health benefits of public housing does not compel elected officials to act. Appealing to the moral conscience of politicians is often like asking our slumlord to fix our sink.

Even organizing, when bent toward the electoral process, has served to undermine our collective power. Since the late 1970s, government austerity has constrained community organizations in the content of their aspirations and the form of their activity. Groups had to provide critical survival services no longer supported by the state and to secure funding through contingent grants and philanthropic foundations.[5] Community organizations professionalized, saddled with the foremost mandate to financially reproduce themselves. Many now privilege symbolic actions and prepacked campaigns to "raise awareness" and pull policy levers.[6] They enlist tenants in struggles for reforms—often doomed to failure without the disciplinary force of an engaged, mass base.[7] The goal of organizing, in this model, is increasing tenants' leverage within existing institutions. Organizing has been reduced to mobilizing—in other words, lobbying without money.

In their everyday lives, tenants are pushed to solve their problems as atomized individuals, clients of social workers and tenant lawyers who will help us negotiate the legal system, accessing what few rights we have, and no more. Of course, this limits tenants to acting within states of personal emergency—after the eviction notice, when we're already in court. It constrains us to adopt concessionary and defensive stances in advance. It forces us to give up our agency to an expert who will do what they can for us. And it forces us to struggle alone.

EVIDENCED IN BOTH the skyrocketing price of rent and the colander of policies we have to protect us, tenants are losing the class war. It is landlords who shape the policies that govern us while they extract rent and evict us. Landlords claim a greater and greater share of what we earn, while we lose our footing in the neighborhoods we helped create. Of course, a view of history as class struggle may be inconvenient. It means the sorry state of things has obtained because we let it. We accepted unjust rent increases. We moved when things got hard. But it also means we can be the ones to change things. We're all we've got, but we're also the ones we've been waiting for.

A tenants union is a vehicle for class struggle. If the work of a tenants association is to coordinate the actions of individual tenants, a tenants union coordinates the actions of those associations and larger groups. The technology is the same. Alone, tenants suffer the whims of our landlords and real estate speculators, who have bent the housing market and the state to their will; together, we discover tools to tip the scales. Isolated, we are objects of a system that prioritizes the people who own our housing over those who live in it; organized, we become subjects of its transformation.

A tenants union treats tenants as experts in their own experience and as agents of the changes we need. Who builds a tenants union? We do. Who is it for? Us. A union allows tenants to claim collective control of our housing and our lives. By organizing ourselves and our neighbors, we change from clients or constituents to creators of our own futures. We don't just gain more leverage within existing institutions; we gain the power to transform those institutions into ones that serve our needs. A union helps us take control over the processes and outcomes of our fights. It connects strategies and tactics across space and time such that our efforts can build in ambition and scale.

Rather than prepare blueprints for an imaginary tenants move-ment, we ground this chapter in how one is already unfolding in Los Angeles, in the LA Tenants Union. This chapter has been shaped by the victories and challenges that have emerged from LATU's nine years of organizing. The union has grown from a single meeting in Hollywood to the largest dues-funded tenants union in the coun-try, a movement of three thousand households, predominantly of working-class, Spanish speaking immigrants and their kids. Our organizing happens at three scales: tenants associations within buildings, local chapters within neighborhoods, and the union that spans the city. Our local chapters are free to develop their own strategies and priorities—their own culture—unique to the geography, demographics, and the individuals who make up each one. Our Northeast Local, for example, focuses on building com-munity and socializing tactics for self-defense; East Hollywood emphasizes militant confrontations with landlords; Union de Vecinos Eastside prioritizes claiming the common space of apart-ments and the neighborhood. Our union benefits from every local experiment. We've won collective bargaining agreements, reversed illegal lock-outs, canceled rent debt, secured building-wide repairs, and defended tenant dignity. Most importantly, we've learned that tenants can intervene in their lives in the present, and that these interventions—even when they end in failure—build momentum for future victories. If our goal is to abolish the power relation of rent, tenant organizing is our only road.

HOW DO WE build a tenants union? We answer with five strategies: we build community, we organize units of power, we reclaim space, we experiment and learn, and we keep the faith. We build relationships of trust and solidarity among neighbors. When we organize such relationships into associations, local chapters, and the citywide union, we create instruments of collective action to change the relationship between our landlords and us. By reclaiming the common space of our buildings and our blocks, we assert ourselves as the stewards of the places where we live. We educate ourselves, acting our way into thinking and archiving past tactics to build an arsenal for the future. Already present in our actions is the seed of a different way of life. Call it faith, *mística*, spirit, or God: we claim that righteous abundance as ours in service of the exploited and the oppressed.

The five practices described in this chapter are both antagonistic and prefigurative: they challenge rent, and they help us build an alternative to it, growing the infrastructures for collective self-defense and self-determination. We organize *against* the extraction of rent and the violence of eviction. We organize *for* and *through* another way of being together, another way of managing housing, land, resources, and our time. Of course, these practices are interdependent; we've pried them apart only for clarity. Enacting the principle of small-d democracy— people's self-governance—the tenants union is an instrument to produce small-c communism—collective control over our housing, our land, and our lives.

TAP ONE FINGER against your opposite hand. This is the sound of one tenant's complaint, seeking resolution by themselves. It's the sound of one singular crisis, in search of an individual solution. Now tap two fingers. This is the sound of neighbors talking, understanding that their issues are better served together, attempting a joint effort to meet their needs under the constraints of daily life. Now tap three fingers. This is the sound of a tenants association, with the power to engage its members' landlord, issue demands, even withhold rent, as a bargaining unit. It is the sound of tables turning, power relations intervened. Tap four fingers. This is the sound of a local chapter, where tenants associations come together to support each other, share strategies and meals, and claim space through our neighborhoods. This is the sound of collective refusal, collective defense. Now clap with all five fingers, your whole hand. This is the sound of the tenants union, where locals come together to scale up and spread out their reach, to strengthen bonds of solidarity across the city. This is the sound of collective transformation.

This is a ritual we performed in Los Angeles in June 2022, at the end of the Autonomous Tenants Union Network's first in-person convention, where LATU hosted twenty-two unions from across the country. Beginning with one finger and ending with five, the volume of our clapping measures the effect of collective effort, the effectiveness of coordination at larger scales. We call it a ritual because it combines solidarity with celebration. When we entrain our bodies and act in unison, we experience the power of working and being together. We call forth the faith in what's not yet present but made possible through our work.

How Do We Build the Union? We Build Community

Inés Alcazar has lived on Flower Drive for over fifty years. Her block of rent-stabilized buildings sits against the 110 freeway, near USC and, now, two sports stadiums. Containing about eighty apartments, all the buildings on her block have been acquired over time by Ventus Group, an investment firm spearheaded by two USC alumni. In 2018 Ventus petitioned the city to demolish the block and redevelop the site, and in 2019 the firm managed to oust the adjacent block of rent-stabilized buildings entirely. Alcazar saw it all: one by one, each of her neighbors on that block accepted buyout deals to leave their homes. None could afford a new place anywhere else in the neighborhood. They'd signed over not just their apartments, but their communities, too.

Alcazar told us that when LATU knocked on her door in 2021, it was like having a prayer answered.[8] She joined organizer David Anthony Albright in getting her block together for a meeting on a paved lot behind one of the buildings. Even at that first gathering, the tenants identified their own isolation as a source of disempowerment: the landlord had given out different information to each tenant; he'd offered them all different amounts of money while calling it the maximum allowed; and he'd told them lies about their neighbors cutting deals to get them to turn on each other. They knew then that keeping their housing meant they'd need to work together. First, they had to get to know each other.

Building community on their block also meant staying separate from elected officials and nonprofits, who cynically deploy the idea of "community" for their own advancement or agenda. Their city councilmember, Curren Price Jr., dodged the tenants' calls while attending the developer's ribbon cuttings. The association discovered that Price had accepted campaign donations from both Ventus Group and its CEO. And in 2019 he'd come under investigation for approving real estate deals for his wife's clients.[9] (In 2023 LA's district attorney charged him with ten counts of embezzlement, perjury, and conflict of interest: for $150,000 in bribes, they said, he'd passed on millions in savings to developers.[10])

They had to steer clear of a nonprofit, too. A community organization had claimed to be helping the tenants who'd lived on the block next to theirs. In fact, it had accepted a $100,000 check from Curren Price's district fund, then shut the tenants out of negotiations, encouraging them into individual buyouts. As Alcazar said of both the government representatives and nonprofits working on the block next door, "They were not working for the people.... They were leading them to negotiate their defeat [with the developer] instead of coming to help them fight to stay in their places."[11] They needed to stay independent—and united. Building community on Flower Drive became a key part of the association's strategy to stay put. As individuals, they would likely face the same fate as the tenants a block away. Together, their fate was their own.

Their tenants association both forged new relationships and gave new meaning to old ones. Some members remarked how little they knew of who lived next door, how "good day" and "good night" was the extent of their communication with people who share a profound aspect of their lives. Now, they've put in nearly four years of sharing space and strategizing. Alcazar has seen the production of community—building one-on-one relationships with individuals, negotiating conflicts, and maintaining a group culture that people want to be in and return to—as necessary labor. Alcazar explicitly connects that labor with their association's capacity for self-defense. "No one is going to be there to defend us. We have to defend ourselves," she said. "Working together as a community, it makes you feel you have this power in you. Like nobody is going to take it away."[12]

When one of the owners attended a Flower Drive Tenants Association meeting, Alcazar explained, he praised the buyout offers as opportunities and argued that the new development would improve the neighborhood—though the tenants would not be able to stay to enjoy it. Their community was revealed in their united

front against him that night: "Don't be harassing us, don't be sending anybody to negotiate.... We're not leaving, we want to stay here
and we want to fight for it," Alcazar summarized. By speaking as
a community, the tenants experienced their power to intervene in
the landlord's plans and take control of the situation. "He said his
truth," Alcazar said, "But his truth was not the truth."[13]

Acting in community remakes our political orientation to
our everyday life. Alcazar explained that participating in the
union has transformed her relationship to the idea of "communism," which she once associated with being controlled. Now, she
says, it's about having control. "Communist to me is community.
Community working together. Common, you have everything in
common. That's communism. My dream is that one day not only
Flower Drive but all these tenants unions become communist—
communist as working together, for one purpose, getting a house
for everybody."[14]

In organizing together, we learn that the living conditions in our
individual apartments are rarely isolated. If our electricity is on the
fritz, the apartments on our line share the same issues. If our sink
leaks, it does so onto the neighbor downstairs. Roaches and rats
are excellent teachers of this truth: they crawl through the spaces
that keep us separate—a problem for one is a problem for all. We
share more than a landlord: we share hallways and yards, parking
lots and alleys, lobbies, trash and laundry rooms. And we share the
physical space of our block. Who is put at risk by a landlord's failure to maintain our buildings? Who gets rats when a landlord fails
to collect trash on time? Our immediate neighbors are implicated

in our struggle. They are also who we have to rely on when we need support. Who can show up the quickest when our landlord tries to harass us or when the sheriffs arrive to throw us out?

A tenants union helps transform groups of people into defensive and offensive communities. Community isn't a resource waiting to be tapped, or a static object ready to be discovered. It isn't a network we access or a system we unveil. Community is an intentional process and a long-term commitment. The meanings of our communities are often shaped by those who seek to exploit them, negotiating defeat in their names. We reject these white-washed notions. Our communities are forged in struggles for tenant power, which put poor and working-class people in control of the institutions in which they participate. Community names our braided relationships, anchored by place and shared activity. As LATU cofounder Dont Rhine often says, "We make our community by defending it."

Alone in our apartments, we are likely to ignore the disrepair of our housing, believing that we should be grateful for the roof over our heads, that nothing would change even if we complained, or that speaking up would make us targets for retaliation. The union builds community to allow tenants to overcome their shame and share their living conditions with each other. Collectively identifying a pattern of neglect, that community helps us find the resolve to intervene and the will to collectivize risk.

WHEN THE HABITS we know are interrupted, when we can no longer swing by a neighbor's house on the way home from work, pick up a snack at our favorite street vendor, recognize the faces of our neighbors, we feel lost, frightened, severed, furious. We no longer experience our homes as ours. We experience what sociologist Mindy Fullilove calls "root shock," a trauma with physical and emotional consequences.[15] The union builds community to overcome this sense of disempowerment, to testify to our ongoing presence in our neighborhoods, to bolster our sense of control over our lives. When we act together in solidarity, we solidify the bonds gentrification breaks.

Our unions are shaped not just by what we're fighting against, but also by what we're fighting for. Grounded in the everyday survival of tenants and the social life of our buildings and communities, they strengthen the practices of mutual care that already existed between us. We build up systems of communication; we guard packages, watch each other's pets and children, run errands for those of us who are sick; we share the burden of child care, provide for each other's basic needs with food distribution and harm reduction, and create spaces for art and celebration. Our unions weaponize everyday life.

Understanding the union as a community helps us clarify who its leaders are: the base members who maintain the relationships that constitute it, who cultivate deep and stable coexistence. We can recognize leadership in those who provide their homes as social spaces, who set up meetings, who make reminder calls, who make sure that everyone feels welcome. Leaders take ownership of collective belonging. For our leaders, there is no separation between the social life of their building, block, and neighborhood and the struggle to stay put. The union is a way of life.

The home is where we reproduce our lives, where we maintain our bodies, where we eat our meals, where we care for our families, our elders, and our social and private selves. But the home has been made a place of private subordination, the place where we're supposed to deal with the fallout of our grueling jobs on our own, manage our disintegrating futures without making a fuss. The tenants union disrupts that project of isolation, politicizing domestic space and challenging the right's current monopoly over visions of what our homes—our reproductive lives—should be like. Of course, domestic space is often maintained by women's unpaid second shift, their labor of caring, cooking, cleaning, and community making. As a movement to defend and control the home, our movement will often be led by women—women on their third shift, performing the labor of social justice. Tenant organizing is domestic work to be carried out by people of all genders. It makes homemaking a project to remake the world.

How Do We Build the Union?
We Organize Units of Power

Early on a Saturday morning in July 2022, about forty people from the East Hollywood local gathered in Lemon Grove Park to support one of their members. They were preparing to deliver their local's "tenant declarations" to her landlord's home. The tenants took turns reading the declarations aloud, beginning, "1. Repairs not made within 15 days will be made by [the] Tenant who will deduct the cost and penal[ize] the following month's rent." Its final sentence read, "We don't need landlords." The tenant reminded the group of the unlivable condition of her apartment: ripped carpets, holes in the drywall, leaks from both of her sinks. Despite her complaints, nothing had been fixed. Together, they made a plan for action and assigned responsibilities. They drove in a caravan to Hancock Park, a wealthy neighborhood four miles away from the tenant's home. They parked their cars and walked silently to the landlord's door. The tenant knocked. No one answered, but the lights inside suggested someone was home. An organizer called the landlord's name through a megaphone. The group chanted. They taped a list of needed repairs and a copy of the tenant declarations to his door. Eventually, they headed back to the park. Days later, quietly, repairs began.

Eviction is personal for us. It should be personal for our landlords too. The East Hollywood local has made it a repeated tactic of their work to name landlords, publicize their neglect, visit their houses, and disrupt their social lives. So many systems protect landlords from having to encounter the consequences of their actions, from the LLCs that anonymize their identities to the physical distance that separates their homes from ours. But as East Hollywood's offensive practices insist, our rights as tenants have not just *been violated*, they *have violators*. Tony Ramirez of the East Hollywood local explained, "We rarely focus on the landlord: who he is, where he lives, what he does with the money that we give him. But we need to know who this person is who takes our wages."[16]

The point of the tenant declarations is to cultivate the antagonism between landlord and tenant: "This is a class issue," Ramirez said. "The landlord is the class enemy of the tenant . . . and the only way tenants can overcome landlords is by confronting them."[17] These protests are not symbolic; they force the landlord to respond. They intimidate. They make the landlord visible to himself and his neighbors. We cross the borders of race and class that segregate the city, refusing to play our part. We get to see firsthand how our landlords benefit from the rent we pay.

When repairs are made after an action, tenants see that organized power produces results. And that we ourselves can act as collective pressure to deliver these results to others. This iterative process composes the grounds of what Ramirez calls the "new, tenant-ruled world," a world without rent.[18] As the declarations say: "We are on a mission to annihilate rent because it never made sense to pay landlords to make our lives miserable."

Organizing is the alchemy—and the science—that turns individualized vulnerability into shared power. When groups of tenants come together against a landlord, they form a "unit of power," to borrow a term from Dr. Martin Luther King Jr. In *Where Do We Go from Here: Chaos or Community?* King argued that spectacular actions and legislative focus, which had characterized the civil rights movement, were not enough to end racial domination. Laws had changed, but lasting transformations of the Jim Crow order, in both the North and South, were elusive. What was needed was durable organization to both enforce the laws and transform the underlying property relations that constrain their scope in advance: the capacity to win not just integration, but redistribution of wealth and power.[19] "To produce change," King, once a tenant organizer himself, wrote, "people must be organized to work together in units of power," including "economic units such as groups of tenants who join forces to form a tenant union or to organize a rent strike."[20] We like the term "units of power" also because "units" are what the real estate industry calls the places where we live. Rather than abstracted, interchangeable containers, our homes are unique and concrete sites of struggle.

In King's time as now, the expected path for organizing is to shift power up and out of local and immediate fights to try to win them at the level of the state. In this model, substantive changes in everyday life trickle down from policy and the law and our role is reduced to passive support for the politicians who might deliver it. But like with our own landlords, we cannot guarantee that we will get the concessions we ask for from the state. Those state powers fiercely guarded by real estate—taxation, regulation, redistribution, expropriation, eminent domain—will only be put to our benefit through mass disruptive constraint. And, as we know from living in broken-down apartments in cities with habitability laws on the books, what laws we win are only as good as their enforcement.

The promise of a tenants union is that by organizing ourselves and our neighbors, we can step into our power as tenants to intervene in and transform the exploitative conditions under which we live—ourselves. A tenants union redistributes power down into our everyday lives to challenge power and property relations directly. It operates at the level of our concrete grievances, our broken pipes and busted appliances. Instead of relying on the law to act on our behalf, we promote disruptive, direct, collective action that concentrates on our immediate antagonist—our landlords—while cultivating grassroots leadership and capacity along the way.

We organize vertically and horizontally, as tenants associations within our buildings (bargaining units) and as local chapters across the space of our blocks and neighborhoods (units of community defense). When a tenants association confronts a single landlord, we coordinate our activity to extract concessions and win our demands by showing up at our landlord's home or place of work, making repairs and deducting the cost from our rents, even withholding our rents in a rent strike. Acting as a unit—in unison—we gain access to something we don't have as individuals: economic and social sanctions. We become the enforcement of the laws we have and can even cement greater protections.

As we work to coordinate our efforts across scales of activity, we use our collective resources to push for immediate—and bigger—victories. Direct action is not just a tactic but a way of organizing that takes a defiant and impatient attitude toward injustice and puts the solutions to our problems into our own hands. In our buildings and beyond, as the rallying cry of the National Union of the Homeless went, "You only get what you're organized to take."

How Do We Build the Union? We Reclaim Space

In early 2004, Mr. Romero, a member of the Fickett Street block committee in Boyle Heights, stepped out of his car into an alley behind Folsom Street. As Romero pried open the gate to his building's garage, he was mugged. The encounter was extreme. He ended up in the hospital. Romero's family didn't want to call the police, fearing reprisals from the local gang, for whom the alley was a regular hangout. Nor did the family believe the police would prevent another incident from occurring. Instead, as Romero rested, his family and a few neighbors decided to investigate what they could do to address the problem themselves.

Rather than focus on the gang members, they started with the place—the conditions of the alley itself. Mr. Romero couldn't see his attackers because they had been hiding in piles of trash: smashed bottles, crinkled wrappers, a busted refrigerator, hunks of bed frames, dressers with their broken drawers strewn across the pavement. So the tenants began by organizing a cleanup, inviting other neighbors that shared the alley to help. Most were skeptical. But, "No hay peor lucha que la que no se hace," they reminded each other. "There is no worse fight than the one that is not done."

The group labored to remove the bulky items and trash. But by the next week, the alley was full of trash again. The alley had become a dump, and the neighborhood used it like one. Disappointed but undeterred, they got together and cleaned it again the next weekend. For the Esperanza Neighborhood Committee of Union de Vecinos, it became a weekly ritual. More buildings joined the effort. Some of the local youth could no longer sit by and watch older women lug trash bags through the streets; they took on some of the effort themselves. Neighbors began to fear angering others should they be caught dumping trash. The conditions—and the purpose—of the alley began to change.

Maria Gomez and her neighbors decided to show a movie in the alley on a summer night. As they were setting up, lining one side of the alley with folding chairs and the other with snacks, a local gang member told her to clear everything out. "What are you doing? This is our alley," Gomez remembers he'd said. She pointed to the families preparing for the show. "It's just a night," she demurred, "We already invited people."[21] When everyone settled and the movie began, Gomez noticed the young man and a few friends watching alongside them. The next weekend, those same men returned. By the next week, they helped redirect traffic, securing the space for the now weekly event. The committee also began to use the alley in the daytime for a craft and food market. They produced a safer, cleaner neighborhood by inhabiting the space they shared. They installed a small flag: "Esta es mi comunidad, yo la limpio, y la cuido." "This is my community, and I clean it, and care for it." Rivaling the tagging used by the gangs to claim territory, they claimed the alley for the community.

The block committees began to pay the same attention to more of the city around them. Their streets lacked lights and crosswalks; the roads were riddled with potholes; the sidewalks had been cracked by roots. All around them was evidence that they had been abandoned by the city, the state, and the feds, while other neighborhoods were full of paved, shaded, tended places. They began to come up with their own solutions: they filled potholes with sand gathered from construction sites; they borrowed tools to iron out streets; they painted their own crosswalks; they staffed their own team of crossing guards outside of local schools; they rolled up discarded rugs and laid them in the street as speedbumps. Resources were scarce, but collective ingenuity wasn't. "Más vale pedir perdón que pedir permiso," they said. "It's better to beg forgiveness than ask permission."

The committee did not give up on making demands of city government, understanding that the state maintained the economic and technical resources to address many of their concerns. The tenants collectively identified their needs and developed the capacity to make use of all available resources to address them—both their own and those of the state. By continuing to take action themselves, they created the authority and the structures of accountability to make demands, not requests. Through their organizing, they forced the city to install stoplights at once-perilous intersections as well as streetlights that now illuminate almost two miles of once-dark alleys. As the block committee has grown, joining the LA Tenants Union when Union de Vecinos became the Eastside local chapter, cleanups have remained a feature of their work—as have parties, movie nights, and food distribution in public space.

The walls of the alleys have now been adorned with several murals. Across First and Soto is a mural of the members of the block committee holding up a banner that reads, "No más aumento de renta, únete a la campaña." "No more rent increases, join the campaign." Wrapping the corner of Evergreen and Ganahl is a cartoon cityscape, lined with the handprints of the children who painted it. A twenty-foot-tall Our

Lady of Guadalupe now guards the alley behind Folsom. Once a space the neighbors feared, many of the alleys have become part of a network of reclaimed public space that grounds community life. Beyond pedestrian passage, the alleys were a road to reclaiming tenants' homes.

One of the most powerful weapons we have as tenants is our physical presence. We take up space. To separate us from our housing—whether an apartment, a car, or a piece of the sidewalk—our landlords have to physically remove us. When we stand in the way of eviction or even of rent collection, occupying our homes becomes an *occupation* of our homes. Similarly, when we reclaim shared spaces—hold association meetings in our lobbies, grow plants in our backyards, repair our sidewalks, clean our alleys, block traffic to host a union party on our street—we *occupy* our buildings, our neighborhoods, and the city. We emphasize the political, social, and cultural fabric of a neighborhood rather than its value as real estate, exercising our movement's "territorial imperative," to use Eldridge Cleaver's phrase.[22] We leverage the spaces of our buildings and neighborhoods as beachheads for building tenant power.

The connection between community improvement and displacement is so routine as to have made an *Onion* headline: "Trees Planted in Poor Neighborhood Mature Just in Time for Gentrification."[23] We want streetlights, public space, and shade. We face dark alleys, potholes, and asphalt. As "good citizens," we make reports to local agencies and ask our representatives to resolve our issues. We navigate websites, fill out forms, and file reports, yet the issues persist. Sometimes, resources arrive, yet by the time they do we're the ones who have to go. Our housing becomes more valuable than our presence; our presence becomes a threat to its value. When we take community improvement into our own hands, we become its agents to ensure that we are its beneficiaries. We get a small taste of what collective control of our neighborhoods and our cities could be like—a reality of the chant, "Whose streets? Our streets!"

As we reclaim our neighborhoods, we develop a deeper understanding of the community we are building and our vision for it. We change our relationships to each other and to the state. Building power to solve our problems ourselves and demanding that the state serve our needs is often framed as a contradiction. Like the Esperanza Committee, we should understand them as interrelated processes: we can both take autonomous action and claim resources, infrastructure, and logistics from the state. Making material improvements to our housing and our neighborhoods grows our power to make and enforce demands. And to win a responsive and transformed state, we need denser, unified organization—countervailing power.

As the Esperanza Committee demonstrates, our unions also work to keep us safe, addressing the coincidence of state abandonment and state violence; the state fails to address the needs of the poor and invests in punishing them instead. Police are not preventative: they arrive only after an event has occurred. They can take information. They can promise to investigate. But they cannot heal a wound, and rarely can they find what was taken. Instead, their presence makes an emergency worse; they heighten drama, hand out tickets, make arrests, harass, even execute. These are the consequences of deputizing our safety to an outside, occupying force: we are fearful of our neighbors, disempowered from handling conflict. We are dependent. And we are less safe.

Organizing as tenants clarifies the function of the police as protectors of property rather than as law enforcement. If a landlord wants to kick us out, the cops arrive to carry it out with brute force—whether legal or not. If your roof caves in or your pipes burst, breaking habitability laws, you wait for weeks for housing inspectors to issue a flimsy complaint. And we know the suspicion that greets us when our neighborhoods "change," what can happen when police decide that we are "out of place" somewhere, even when we've lived there our whole lives. If it's the relations of private property, not our safety, that police exist to protect, fighting against rent will inevitably set them against us, and us against them.

But our unions can work to make policing irrelevant. Practicing self-organized safety connects the abolition of rent to the abolition of police and prisons: we make the local infrastructures we need to keep each other safe without cops and cages.[24] Our safety comes from neighbors knowing each other, helping each other, and protecting each other. By bringing tenants into democratic institutions over which we all have a say, we cut off the recruitment strategy for "law and order" politics, which capitalize on our sense of a loss of control. By taking control of our disinvested spaces, we don't just respond to the violence in our neighborhoods, we prevent it. We make spaces safe by making them useful to us—as the alley behind Folsom Street was lit with new lights, monitored by mothers selling crafts, and cleaned by community volunteers. A safe space is an inhabited space.

How Do We Build the Union?
We Experiment and Learn

K3 Holdings owns at least forty-one properties in Los Angeles.[25] A family business, the company is owned by Nathan, Joshua, and Michael Kadisha (the three Ks), who are nephews of billionaire Neil

Kadisha, founder of Omninet Capital, which controls more than thirteen thousand apartments in the US.[26] K3's business model is simple: they acquire large, rent-stabilized buildings and target long-term tenants for displacement and replacement. Rent-stabilized apartments remain the largest source of stable housing for the poor and working class of Los Angeles: stabilization limits rent increases, guarantees lease renewals, and prevents arbitrary eviction. However, under California law, if a stabilized apartment is vacated, a landlord can reset the rent at any price. As rents rise over time—that is, as landlords raise rents—the gap widens between what long-term tenants pay and what a landlord could claim on their apartments without them in the way.

K3 starts with legal means to remove rent-stabilized tenants: the "voluntary vacate" offer, often called "cash-for-keys." Of course, "voluntary" does not accurately describe K3's deals—predation and harassment are the norm. K3 relies on a burgeoning eviction industry, hiring so-called re-tenanters to pressure long-term residents into accepting lowball deals. Re-tenanters Matt DeBoth and Angel Escobar use English-only notices as well as bunk legalese to enact discriminatory campaigns against K3's Spanish-speaking residents, accost tenants at all hours of the day and night, and escalate with threats and lies. "They have a playbook of certain lies they tell people," Sam Trinh, K3 resident and LATU organizer, told us.[27] K3's representatives claim that vacate offers will expire (they often don't), or that the building will be demolished (it won't), that the tenants will be evicted whether they accept the offer or not (they can't be). When tenants have refused, re-tenanters have threatened to call immigration enforcement.

According to Los Angeles Department of Housing data analyzed by journalist Jack Ross, K3 made 167 buyouts between July 2019 and January 2021, spending more than $4.3 million to remove long-term, rent-stabilized tenants from their homes.[28] Exposed records put the tally of deals much higher: 545 apartments. We know of former K3 tenants now living in cars and surfing on couches, unable to secure market-rate housing with their buyouts. After being ejected from his rent-stabilized apartment, one became ill and passed away.

Not all K3 tenants would leave. Across eight buildings, both long-term and newer residents have formed associations within their buildings and organized themselves into the K3 Tenant Council, which spans them all. K3 organizing shows us the pedagogical function of the tenants union in microcosm: how information is shared, how tactics are tested, and how that feedback process contributes to the growth and strength of the movement.

"You can actually look at other buildings and, say, oh, that building is where we were ten months ago, or, oh, that building is where we're gonna be in two months," Trinh said. Besides encountering the same patterns in re-tenant harassment, K3 tenants also experience the same response if they refuse to leave: "I call it the K3 embargo. They just don't fix anything." K3's refusal to make repairs occurs simultaneously with another harassment tactic: renovations. Many of these renovations are unpermitted and unsafe, sending noise at all hours and construction debris from blasted ceilings and busted pipes into the homes of remaining residents. Renovations perform two functions, flipping the homes of displaced tenants for higher-paying ones and tormenting those who remain. These common experiences are part of the council's self-definition. "There's the bubble that shows up on people's walls: it's like, dirty liquid. That's part of the K3 lore. Also the moldy carpet thing. It's a symbol of what K3 puts us through."[29]

The K3 Tenant Council affirms K3's malign neglect, even when the state agencies tasked with intervening will not. When Trinh called to support another member of the council during a REAP hearing (a process by which repeat code violators are sanctioned by the Housing Department), the arbiter of the hearing dismissed Trinh's testimony as irrelevant because he lived in a different building from the one discussed. "What is happening in this building is the same shit they do. Like this is the same people," Trinh recalled.[30] But the housing department quarantined K3 buildings from each other, refusing to see the repetition as evidence of a wider pattern. The K3 Tenant Council opposes this disorganization by bringing together K3 tenants from across the city to match K3's own scale.

Strategies of fighting back travel among associations in the tenant council. Each building doesn't have to invent tenant organizing from scratch. Alma Angel was one of the first K3 tenants to join LATU and fight back against K3, defending her home of twenty-three years. A Spanish speaker with two children, Angel refused buyout offers of $21,000, $40,000, then finally $100,000. When renovations began in the other apartments in her building, she demanded she receive repairs, too. Even after two decades of living in her apartment, her carpet had never been replaced. Frayed sections revealed swelling patches of mold. Re-tenanter Angel Escobar told Angel she could either accept her apartment as is, or accept a buyout. Instead, she gathered with her neighbors, interrupting construction to demand workers rip up her carpet. They agreed, forcing the landlord to replace it once and for all.

The K3 council archives tactics of resistance, remixes them for new contexts, and proliferates them across its membership. Trinh explains, "The thing is, we can just recycle. Like the mold battles from four or five tenants. One of the first ones is Alma; [her struggle was] the first of everything. That's how we learn. She invented a strategy, now that's how we know how to get things done."[31] Angel's struggle created a blueprint for the rest of the council. Indeed, her testimonial is now featured in the hand-out LATU organizers use when canvassing about "cash-for-keys" across the city.

As tenants share successes and failures, they inspire others to try the same thing and push even further for the conditions they deserve. In their statement of demands and origins, the K3 council describes this process: tenants associations "reflected back their power to one another—informing each other of victories, encouraging each other not to back down, asking each other for support—and this process of mutual reflection created a sort of amplification, building the [association's] confidence, opening up possibilities for even bolder actions and demands."[32]

The council produces a culture of experimentation that encourages political risks. "I was the crash dummy," Trinh said about his own eviction case, which led him into organizing. "I was the guinea pig of the whole council. . . . It's like alright, let's see what happens to Sam. That's gonna tell us everything about K3's weaponry."[33] In the fight against landlords, outcomes are not known in advance, and winning is not guaranteed. Framing an eviction case as an occasion for learning and experimentation is a challenging spin on what could mean the loss of a home. This is a pedagogical orientation to taking tenant power.

As our unions create spaces for reflection, we practice popular education. Experiments and experiences travel, get repeated as success stories and cautionary tales, and amplify each other. We carry forward the strategies of our elders, transmitting movement and organizing knowledge across generations. A tenants union is a school where tenants use our own actions as a source of learning. And through that learning, we move to act on—meaning, in small and larger ways change—the world.

No one is more capable of recognizing the injustice of rent and the need for the transformation of our housing system than poor and working-class tenants. At the same time, the knowledge of injustice is not built into the experience of living through it. Nor is the knowledge of how to end that injustice. Popular education is an orientation to organizing that facilitates the self-conscious activity of poor and working-class tenants and puts poor and working-class tenants in control of the process of liberation. If we assign to the poor and working class the power to change the world, they must be the leaders of our struggle.

Popular education has often been severed from its political context. Brazilian educator Paulo Freire's critique of the "banking" model of education (in which students are treated as empty vessels to be filled with a teacher's knowledge) reflects a broader challenge to the imperial project, in which the global north is believed to improve the global south by injecting investment—and subjecting it to its management.[34] For Freire, a liberatory struggle necessarily involves learning: it's not a script into which the poor and working class are cast. "Attempting to liberate the oppressed without their reflective participation in the act of liberation is to treat them as objects that must be saved from a burning building," he wrote.[35] Septima Clark, Ella Baker, and Miles Horton popularized this method in the US South, centering poor Black workers as the protagonists of the Black freedom struggle.[36] Popular education relies on the capacities of poor and working-class people to name the conditions that constrain their lives and to reflect on the tactics they can use to reshape those conditions themselves.[37]

To understand the union as a school, we might need a different orientation toward organizing from what we're used to. Often those who call themselves "organizers," as Dont Rhine notes, are those who can leave—the building, the neighborhood, the conditions of survival that make organizing a necessity. We see no reason to shy away from the designation of "outside agitator" to name those pulled from the ranks of the downwardly mobile middle class or even upper-class traitors. Solidarity is a shared stake in liberation for us all. At the same time, a pedagogical organizer—pulled from any background—must have the humility to support the leadership of our base. Rather than paid professionals or activists bringing the "good news" to the poor and working class, conscripting their participation into campaigns with predetermined goals, organizing must be a process of listening, problem posing, and facilitating self-driven activity.

LATU's 2022 annual assembly gathered hundreds of members to collectively reflect on our work in a popular education process we called "Naming the Moment."[38] Through this process, our members encountered excerpts from recorded interviews with other members, articulating our struggle in their own words. In groups, they responded to the question, "What are we actually doing in our union to work towards the question posed in the assembly's theme, 'Block by Block: Towards a World Without Rent'?" One key moment from an interview continued to stand out to the organizing committee. As Lucia Chappell said of the Kent Tenants Association: "We always looked out for each other. You know, always if I hollered out the window, I knew somebody would come. That's how we've always been. And that's the kind of world I want to live in. . . . Sometimes you can be that way, but unless you have a name for it, like 'tenants association' or 'neighborhood group' or something like that, other people don't realize that that's how you are. And unless other people realize that, it can't become contagious."[39]

Chappell's statement is an injunction to take seriously the social function of our tenants associations. More than just a bargaining unit, they are a way to ground social life. For her, a tenants association names how a building takes care of each other, brings intention to being in community. But Chappell also names the purpose of popular education: it's how we name our practices so they might spread.

How Do We Build the Union? We Keep the Faith

The three wise men, Mary, and Joseph converge on the corner of Seventh and Lucas, appointed with fake beards, long robes, and signs. They're surrounded by a larger group wearing red. Just before Christmas 2016, the Vermont y Beverly local chapter staged an action at the offices of the LA Housing Department, the city agency tasked with inspecting code violations, mediating conflicts between tenants and landlords, approving "cash-for-keys" deals, and instructing tenants on their rights. The action took the shape of a Posada, which, in the Mexican tradition, reenacts Mary and Joseph's search for shelter. Congregants sing a song in which a place to rest is sought and denied, sought and denied, then finally granted. By seeking shelter at the Housing Department, the local chapter called attention to the failures of LAHD to keep tenants in their homes: LAHD officials had been rubber-stamping temporary relocation requests, banishing tenants from rent-stabilized homes to locations that did not even exist—in one instance, the tenants had been assigned to a cemetery. By remixing the Posada, LATU members, the majority of whom are immigrants who participate in faith-based organizations, shared their traditions with the political project of the union. The action leveraged that righteousness in service not of a specific religion or denomination, but of protest.

Political risks are more than strategic vision; they are acts of faith. "In biology, one learns about a certain species of caterpillar that can only cross the threshold of metamorphosis by seeing its future butterfly," writes Mike Davis. A movement "does not evolve by incremental steps but requires non-linear leaps . . . [through the work of] non-utilitarian actors, whose ultimate motivations and values arise from structures of feeling that others would deem spiritual."[40] A tenants union is a spiritual, not a professional, enterprise—even a church. We don't mean this because we share a religion, but because our unions help us develop and sustain a relationship to something greater than ourselves, something we don't yet know is possible, something we commit to whether or not we see the fruits of our work.

SEE HIS BEADY eyes and his beak. See his mass of fur. See his stooping neck, from which hangs an impossibly long red tie. He carries an eviction notice and a bag of cash. He is LATU's seven-foot puppet: a figure of a Vulture Landlord. The Vulture Landlord walks beside us at marches and shows up at landlords' houses. Both goofy and serious, he is an immediately recognizable symbol of a collective analysis. Like a vulture eats the dead, the landlord takes what we earn. Alongside him we chant, "Vulture landlord, get a real job!"

Transforming reality is an unmistakably creative project. It demands imagination, experimentation, improvisation. It takes a sense of play. In our union, we engage in what Brazil's Landless Workers' Movement (MST) calls mística—performances, rituals,

symbols, and celebrations that sustain the struggle.[41] Mística lets us
flex our creativity for each other, keep up our spirits, and draw others
into our work. It helps us sense that we are building in the present
the seed of a future we want. We roleplay: we practice one-on-ones,
how to knock on our neighbor's doors. We use performance: for
the discussion about the challenges of our work at the 2022 LATU
annual convention, for instance, the facilitators threw participants
a curve; instead of speaking their report-backs, they were asked to
perform them as a skit. We integrate the traditions of faith into our
actions as material: for our yearly Day of the Dead action, we constructed an altar for all of those we had lost in struggle. An action is
more than an action: it is ceremony, liturgy. Endowed with meaning through repetition, meetings themselves are rituals, in which
union business is an occasion for the pleasure of being together, and
eating together becomes breaking bread.

Participation in collective action rests on shared collective
identity, shared investment in the collective project of tenant struggle. We are no longer ashamed of our living conditions or having to
ask for help; we are angry. What before seemed natural and inevitable, something to be assumed and accepted, becomes injustice,
evidence of an unfair system and a world gone awry. A union forges
solidarity and collective identity by maintaining a culture that
opposes dominant values, calling on a higher authority than capitalism and the state. Against the sense of loss and depression that
comes with the violence of gentrification, a union cultivates pride
and dignity. Against individuation, mutuality. Against competition, solidarity. Against the system that profits off a basic human
need, the abolition of rent. Our doctrine is the agency of everyday
people to change the conditions of their everyday lives. We believe
that by building lasting infrastructures of collective control, we can

crowd out the power of landlords and developers, shape our homes and our neighborhoods to our needs. We believe that organized tenants have an essential contribution to make in reordering the world, that practicing new forms of collective struggle will chart the course to new forms of collective life.

HOW DO YOU resolve the tension between the emergency we are living through and the fact that the only tools we have to work with— organizing and collective action—take so much time? How do you continue to fight when our members lose—lose their homes, their cases, and sometimes even their lives? How do you produce a relationship to something that we don't know is possible, that has never yet existed? The union is what makes it possible to continue in the face of all the conditions that made it seem like the rational thing to do would be to give up.

We work upon the world, and we ourselves are changed by doing so.[42] We experiment with strategies that intervene in our material reality and find communion with a movement of tenants, a purpose to our work greater than the sum of its parts, an intergenerational commitment for building a future unlike our present, a future worthy of us and of our love. We see that collective organization can transform structures that we inherit as natural and think will be eternal. We find that our reality is plastic. On a daily basis, we consent to its making and being remade. In other words, its transformation is in our hands; it's up to us to work together to make the reality we want *real*.

"As long as I fight, I am moved by hope; and if I fight with hope, then I can wait," Freire writes.[43] When we affirm, week after week, that what is not yet here is nonetheless possible, when we take concrete steps to a utopian future we may not ourselves live to enjoy, we show commitment—and, unmistakably, our faith. As Inés Alcazar of Flower Drive said of our struggle, "And this, I know, this started long, long ago. And the people that come after us will even go farther. . . . Other people have looked for the land. Other people have removed dirt. And now it's time to start planting the seeds. And other people are going to come and water the seeds, and other people might collect the fruits, so that still other people can eat them."[44]

CHAPTER 5

FROM HOUSING STRUGGLE TO LAND STRUGGLE

"The most radical thing I ever did was stay put."
—Grace Lee Boggs

IN 1962, AT just fourteen years old, Isabel Garcia arrived in Los Angeles from Mexico. She moved straight into her aunt's apartment, a corner of a two-story Craftsman on East Second Street in Boyle Heights. For years, she was surrounded by family, sharing the apartment with her aunt and her sister. As she grew up, her neighbors became family too. She took over the lease. With the help of a local midwife, she gave birth to a son in that same apartment. As she aged, she moved downstairs. In her nearly sixty years as a tenant, three landlords have owned her building. Garcia remains.

As a teenager, Garcia planted two trees in the backyard of her building: a loquat and an avocado. She always loved to work in the garden. Every day when she came home from work, she would tend to the yard, water potted flowers, sweep the path she and her neighbors had etched into the dirt and lined with stones. "If that tree could speak!" Yesenia, Garcia's niece, exclaimed. "One tree was my swimming pool. The other was my swing."[1]

In 2010, a new landlord, Bruce Terani, purchased her apartment and the seven others in her building. Soon, the harassment began. Rent stabilization protected Garcia from rent increases, but not from incessant cash-for-keys offers—for $5,000, he claimed, she could travel the world or secure a spot in a retirement home. He issued repeated three-day "cure or quit" notices—one because she'd left a table in the hallway to make way for an inspection he'd required. He removed the building's shared amenities—washing machines, clotheslines, slop sinks—and installed a five-foot wooden box in the laundry room where there had once been space enough for a table. He began targeting her son with nuisance complaints for hanging out on the stoop where he'd grown up.

Garcia's total rent has likely equaled the cost of the entire building. She understands the injustice: "I have paid for everything, and I still don't have it."[2] For more than a decade, she's had to fight to keep her housing. While battling diabetes, high blood pressure, and heart disease, she has endured a combination of eviction threats and negligence—harassment and abandonment—to stay put. But those conditions have drawn her closer to her neighbors than ever before. In 2020, at the start of the pandemic, Garcia joined a tenants association in her building. She decided to withhold half her rent in solidarity with those who could no longer afford to pay at all.

Garcia can name every past owner of the building. For decades, she could name every nearby neighbor on the block. Her memory and her relationships testify not to the receding history of the neighborhood but to its present: made by its inhabitants, not by its property owners. Though legal documents may suggest property is permanent and tenancy transient, Garcia demonstrates that the opposite is true.

The trees Garcia planted now tower over the two-story house. They bear enough fruit for anyone who asks. They give shade for her neighbors to pass the time together, for weekly tenants association meetings and other events. Every other Tuesday, the building hosts a food distribution in the garden. Residents pack and hand out bags of fresh produce and pantry staples to everyone who attends—about forty thousand pounds and ten thousand bags of food so far. When the Autonomous Tenants Union Network held its first convention in June 2022, drawing together members of twenty-two unions from across the country, we held our party at her house, taking over the yard and the block out front. "We fight," Garcia said, "because we have to continue living." If left to flourish, the trees will outlive us all.

But recently, the garden has become a site of attack. Just before Christmas in 2022, the landlord hired workers to plant two haphazard rows of plants in the center of the space and enclose it with a shoddy, shin-high fence. Only a narrow, circuitous path connected the building to its trash bins. The garden could be looked at, but not entered. As one worker admitted to a resident, the point was to prevent them from being there at all. The plants they installed were evidence of this fact: cacti lined with spikes and pencil trees, whose sap is poisonous, known to cause blisters and rash.

Attacks on tenant gardens are a routine response to our organizing. That these attacks provide no direct financial benefit to the landlord—they often cost money—helps us understand the threat these communal spaces pose. Our landlords want to limit our gardens, our yards, even our lobbies to mere amenities, value propositions to be recruited into the price of our rents and reclaimed in increased extraction. But they are features of our buildings' communal life. They allow us to inhabit our housing together, beyond the commodity the landlord supposedly provides: not just a place to live, but a home; not just a residence, but a community; not just isolated apartments, but a shared base of mutual care, defense, and militancy.

To the people who own and speculate on real estate, our housing is an abstract entity on a balance sheet, an interchangeable "unit," judged according to its performance as an asset. To them, our neighborhoods are just financial opportunities to store and grow their wealth. But tenants turn these spaces into places where we belong. We, after all, are human beings, whose needs for support, rest, and connection have always exceeded the market's ability to incorporate them. We care for our apartments, beautify them—even despite injunctions against doing so. We establish routines etched into our neighborhood and come to rely on our neighbors. We grow attached. We put down roots. Tenant gardens can make these roots literal. When tenants collectively organize how space is used, we challenge private property as its sole governing force.

Collective stewardship is an affront to the legal and economic confines of the rent relation. It is a claim of collective sovereignty, a promissory note our movement may one day cash. Landlords, and the repressive apparatus of the state, understand this implicitly: the threat of tenants making our housing ours is that we will take our housing back.

In this chapter we focus on the already existing practices in the tenant movement that demonstrate this revolutionary horizon. We tell two stories, of the housed tenants of Hillside Villa in Chinatown and the unhoused tenants of Echo Park Lake. The first is a struggle against "affordable housing" (a deceiving, technical term we'll describe soon), the second against carceral housing and the criminalization of living outside. These struggles reflect unique conditions of tenancy, each with divergent histories and distinct legal rights. But both reflect the contradictions of a state under the thumb of real estate. They reveal our current housing crisis as a graveyard of so-called solutions to the housing crisis, where, nonetheless, tenants are working together, struggling for life. And they share strategy and demands: building relationships with each other to stay put in the places we call our homes and taking over common and public space to transform our relationships with our landlords and the state. Both are forms of tenant occupations.

Tenant occupations challenge landlords directly: they confront their power to collect rent and their power to evict. And they challenge real estate's capture of the capitalist state: they confront the powers of policy and those of the police. Of course, for now, collective sovereignty is an aspirational horizon. These occupations are temporary: not final expropriation, but a few years of organized, if uncertain, peace. Even in defeat, they point us toward ways of interacting with the system we currently have to get the system we desperately need.

IF A TENANT is anyone who doesn't control their own housing, then the tenant movement works to establish collective control. Our aim is not to eliminate tenancy by becoming owners ourselves—an impossible prospect whose promise is an engine for our competition and denigration. Our aim is to eliminate the conditions that bind tenancy to insecurity, impermanence, predation, and price gouging. Now tenants are subjected to expulsion and exclusion, gentrification and social cleansing. Financialization dematerializes our homes into flows of capital; monopolization puts them into fewer and fewer hands. But already immanent to everyday tenant struggles is the possibility and practice of another way of governing the places where we make our lives. The ends of the tenant movement will not be an improvement of the exploitative conditions under which we now live, but a wholesale transformation of the social relations that make those conditions possible. As these two struggles demonstrate, rent abolition is a practice of occupation and a process of socialization. The tenant struggle is a land struggle. It is a struggle for collective sovereignty over the use of our resources and the places we inhabit.

The question of managing and governing land sits at the heart of capitalist property relations. How should we divvy up the parcels of our spinning planet, which floats miraculously in space? Whose needs and desires should determine who has access to that limited resource? What is the system that governs how those questions are answered? The actions of tenants already in struggle insist that the solution to our current crisis will not arrive just by building new, publicly owned buildings, but by building power to take back and control public space and the private housing we live in now.

Also revealed in these struggles is our movement's complex relationship to the state, that hostile yet useful amalgam of capacities and resources that we cannot yet guarantee will be put to our use.[3] The state currently organizes land and territory for the purpose of private accumulation. It is the final guarantor of private property and holds a monopoly on violence to protect that property. The state maintains the social relationship between landlords and tenants, ensures our exploitation and domination, even as our movements pressure it to change and reform. Thus, the struggle for the collective control of land will often set us against the state's plans for how land is organized—and how the population of tenants is managed and controlled.

But as we contest capitalist management of space, we contest and remake the capitalist state too. We insist that land use is not a mere technical or economic but a social and political problem, which means it is about how people get together to exercise power. This is a strategic orientation that privileges autonomous organizations and institutions, the practice of taking responsibility for our collective selves. It is neither state-phobic nor state-philic. It views the state as a terrain where resources are often more available to our enemies than to us, but one that we can—and we must—constrain to our will. It understands the history of reforms as concessions to revolutionary social movements and liberation as a project beyond rights, which achieves rights in its wake.

When housed and unhoused tenants practice collective steward-ship of housing and of our public spaces, we wage an offensive against the claims of private landowners and the force of the state. When housed and unhoused tenants refuse to be subordinate actors on the land, we refuse the logic by which financial value is prioritized over human use. This is the liberatory horizon of tenant struggle, a horizon to which we draw closer with our daily work. In a capitalist system, all architecture is hostile architecture. But through building and seizing collective tenant power, we make our housing, our neighborhoods, and the world our home. In this chapter, tenants plant the seeds not just of a collective garden, but of another way of life.

Affordable Housing: Hillside Villa Is Our Place, We Will Not Be Displaced

In October 2018, Leslie Hernandez stood in the hallway of Hill-side Villa, a stucco and concrete complex home to 124 households, trying to communicate with her neighbor Benson Lai, a Canton-ese speaker in his early sixties. Bilingual in English and Spanish, Hernandez turned to her hands. She held up an official notice of a rent increase that had been given to tenants throughout the build-ing and tore it in half. Then she took the pieces and tore those too. When Lai nodded in response, Hernandez knew she had started something. Soon, she'd call it a tenants association.

Though privately owned, Hillside Villa was developed through a combination of state-subsidized loans and tax breaks, tied to a thirty-year covenant to keep rents low.[4] But that covenant ran out in 2018. The landlord, Tom Botz, wanted to see rent doubled.

THE PRIMARY ANSWER the state provides to the permanent crisis of housing is not public housing, owned and operated by the state, nor rent control, which regulates the amount of rent that private land-lords can collect, but privately owned, publicly subsidized housing. Housing Choice Vouchers, also known as Section 8, deliver federal resources to private landlords by picking up the often vast difference between what tenants can afford and market-rate rents. Affordable housing underwrites apartment construction; the government sub-sidizes the cost of development in exchange for establishing, for a limited time, moderate restrictions on rents.[5]

Section 8 serves only one-fourth of those who qualify for it; tenants can wait a decade just to get on the waitlist, then years to get a voucher, then even fail to get a landlord who will agree to take it. Thousands apply for every crop of "Affordable" spots, the major-ity of which go to the middle class rather than the poor.[6] To serve poor and working-class tenants, the state often has to combine both forms of subsidy.[7] Both programs exclude undocumented residents, and tenants risk losing access if they get more work or a partner. The programs funnel public resources into the pockets of private landlords, inflating the price of rent. This means they don't just undermine their own budgets, they undermine tenants everywhere.

Since it was built at the edge of Chinatown in 1989, Hillside Villa has been home to tenants whose rents are subsidized by Section 8, restricted by an affordable housing covenant, or both. In 2018, Hillside Villa was thrust into crisis based on affordable housing's most obvious failure: its rent covenants expire. The landlord was free to kick out all affordable housing tenants and collect market-rate rents in perpetuity. The public benefits were temporary loans; the private gains would be permanent. For almost five years, with the support of organizers from LATU and Chinatown Community for Equitable Development, Hillside Villa tenants have been organizing in three languages—English, Spanish, and Cantonese—to stay put.[8]

SKILLED ORGANIZERS PRACTICING simultaneous interpretation allowed neighbors to communicate with each other across language differences. But as many in the building recall, the main barrier wasn't language, race, or age, but the different forms of tenancy. When the covenant ran out, those in affordable housing would be instantly subject to the whims of the market: their leases would convert to market rate, with no restrictions on rent increases or guarantees for lease renewals. The Section 8 tenants would get rent increases too, but they wouldn't experience them, since the government would pick up the difference. They'd been separated from their economic and political leverage, unable to withhold rent to press for repairs and still fearful of jeopardizing their vouchers,

which kept many of them in the city and from a life outdoors. Those
relying on combining programs had an uncertain mess of bureau-
cracy to wade through. The Hillside Villa Tenants Association rep-
resents not just trilingual organizing but trilegal organizing.

But the tenants had years of history to draw on in forming
their association. Marina Maalouf has lived in the building for
twenty-five years. She raised three children there, watching them
grow alongside the plants she'd planted in the building's central
courtyard: papaya, guava, chilis, avocado, herbs, rue for teas, and
an "insulin plant" to treat diabetes. Adela Cortez, a cancer survivor
now on disability, has also lived in Hillside Villa for more than two
decades, relying on doctors and family close by. Leslie Hernandez
has lived there since she was five years old. Knowing her neighbors
since she was a child made them family. She explained, "To see
them hurting hurts me."[9]

The tenants also built their association through a shared sense
of injustice. Researching their landlord, the tenants discovered
that Botz had an ownership stake in at least five other buildings in
Southern California, with more than 150 apartments in total. They
estimated the value of his home at $3.5 million.[10] Ten years before,
they learned, a California district judge had determined that one
of his companies had systematically discriminated against families
with kids.[11] They also shared deteriorating living conditions. What
were their government subsidies paying for? Their broken elevators,
leaking pipes, roaches. Where was the money going? Tom Botz's
Malibu mansion.

As the Hillside Villa tenants began to meet weekly, working
through the language and legal divides, they watched new developments crop up across Chinatown, some advertising a small percent-
age of "Affordable" apartments like theirs. "Affordable for who?"

Hernandez balked.[12] In Los Angeles, a single person making up to $66,750 a year—more than double the salary of a minimum-wage worker—could qualify.[13] New affordable housing is thus helping to reshape Chinatown and displace its long-time residents, poor and working-class Chinese and Latinx people like them.[14] Leslie recognized the destruction in the process of gentrification: "Chinatown isn't Chinatown anymore." The tenants of Hillside Villa had shared not just a communal life in their building, but decades in the neighborhood. They wanted to remain a part of Chinatown's future.

THE GROUP'S FIRST action was a collective letter that announced the formation of their association and demanded a meeting with their landlord. The letter focused not just on the rent increases, but on the landlord's attacks against the building's communal life: "Our children used to be able to play outside in the common areas, now they are forbidden. . . . We never had armed security, now we have a rent-a-cop who routinely interrogates us, despite knowing who we are."[15] It took months for Botz to agree to meet. When he finally arrived, as tenants recall, he stood cross-armed by their courtyard wall and insisted on his rights to collect market-rate rent. As he'd later reiterate to the press, he had no plans to "coddle" tenants who'd already "been subsidized for thirty-two years."[16] Management retaliated by ignoring the maintenance requests of households who'd organized.

Their lawyers exploited errors in the landlord's rent increase notices, and the tenants made it through more than a year without losing their homes.[17] But by the spring of 2019, no longer content with buying time, Hillside Villa expanded their focus from the landlord to the state. The tenants affirmed to each other that they wouldn't be going anywhere; they'd have to evict their landlord instead. They demanded that the city buy the building and sell it back to them to be held in common. Should their landlord resist, they said, the city should use eminent domain to force the sale.[18]

Their own biographies guided their strategy. Thirty-four years ago, three separate households of current residents had been forced to relocate to Hillside Villa. They'd each been ejected from their homes in downtown Los Angeles when the city used eminent domain to clear their rent-stabilized buildings to make way for the Los Angeles Convention Center. Inaugurated with millions in government subsidies and resulting in the mass displacement of poor and working-class tenants of color, the convention center reflects the policy paradigm of private speculation and property-value inflation, of which affordable housing itself is a part. As Adela Cortez explained, city officials had helped her secure a new apartment in Hillside Villa, but no one told her she was trading permanent protections for temporary ones.[19] The association wanted the city to use eminent domain to protect the same people that power had abused.

At first their city council representative, Gil Cedillo, "wouldn't give them the time of day," Hernandez said.[20] So for months they staked out his office and itinerary, disrupting his events and demanding he meet with them. Their goal was to exploit the councilmember's dependence on a tenant-majority constituency and the landlord's financial dependence on state subsidy, which included not just regular federal transfers from Section 8, but the city's own funds that had financed the building in the first place. The tenants were about to lose their housing, but the landlord was still paying off his city loans.

Finally, the councilmember relented. But rather than accept the association's plans, he offered Botz another deal: $12.7 million in forgiven debt to extend the building's rent caps for ten years.[21]

For a week, the tenants thought they'd won a decade of relief. Then the landlord denied he'd ever made a deal. As he told Fox 11 at the time, government efforts to protect Hillside Villa made him "feel like I'm in Cuba or Venezuela or Sudan but certainly not the United States."[22] Botz urged the city to secure Section 8 vouchers for the tenants at risk of eviction, a program he praised for delivering subsidized rents "like clockwork." Understanding the constraints of the voucher system, Hernandez translated, "'Just go on Section 8' is landlord for 'fuck you.'"[23]

The first wave of eviction filings made it clear: the tenants' presence in their homes stood in the way of their landlord's profits. They relied on legal challenges to protect themselves from getting thrown out, spun on a yo-yo of dread and relief. Botz continued his threats. They continued to organize. In January 2020, Councilman Cedillo introduced a tepid council motion supporting state purchase of their building: a feasibility study.[24] Meanwhile, the association took their struggle to the landlord's door. They walked the streets of Malibu, shouting chants written by Hillside resident Alejando Gutiérrez: "Hillside Villa is our place, we will not be displaced!"

The coronavirus pandemic sent members of the association into further precarity. The landlord sent new eviction notices. Marina Maalouf was laid off from her job. Immunocompromised and at further risk, Adela Cortez stretched disability checks. Leslie Hernandez struggled to find work. Two elderly residents died of the virus. But the city's emergency eviction moratorium brought the tenants a reprieve. It also brought them closer with members of the LA Tenants Union in a demand to cancel—not subsidize—the rent.

In October 2020, rather than continue paying rent for the privilege of being threatened with eviction and denied repairs, a first group of tenants decided it was time to go on rent strike. They could deprive Botz of not just the raised rents he sought, but the rents they were already paying. By February 2021, the rest of the association joined them. Despite the insecurity of the pandemic and their futures, the tenants got a taste of housing that wasn't just "affordable" but free. In holding up rent extraction by staying put, tenants turned occupying their homes into an occupation.

Taking on two targets at once, the tenants staged a series of actions politicizing the city budget—that skeleton of the municipal state. Outside Disney's Concert Hall, they enumerated the tax breaks given to developers that had underwritten that project. At LAPD headquarters, they denounced LAPD's $3.15 billion annual budget, which captures more than a quarter of the city's spending in a year.[25] And in front of City Hall, LA's Housing Department, and the homes of city councilmembers, they listed the hundreds of millions made available to the city through federal pandemic relief.

Finally, in May 2022, under the mounting pressure of an all-union campaign, LA City Council voted to support the purchase of Hillside Villa—in part. The hours of public comment staged a contest of rights, between Botz's "right to begin earning his full return on investment" and the tenants' right to a home.[26] One of Botz's lawyers argued that to take the building away would create a "chilling effect on any developer ever trusting the city again to live up to its end of the bargain when constructing Affordable Housing," a threat of capital strike.[27] As the real estate industry knows, public-private partnerships give the industry, not constituents, disciplinary power over the state.[28] The city voted to purchase the building, but refused to rule on eminent domain. Thus, it continued to avoid the largest impediment to that process: the landlord's refusal to sell.

IN JULY 2022, the landlord retaliated against their win: he hired a crew to destroy the garden in their courtyard.[29] When the crews arrived, they began to tear out the plants and even decades-old trees from their roots, preparing to pour concrete into the beds. Their orders were to rip everything out, with no plans for replacement. Rosa Hernandez explained, "They just want to bother us, because we're taking the building away." Any work on the building, she said, should "go to making the apartments livable."[30] The next day, the tenants organized a picket line to block the contractors from continuing. The building manager called the police. But the picket worked: the crew didn't take up their tools.

A fight between landlords and tenants was again waged over a garden, a contest between the appropriation of common space as amenity and as something more—a communal base of care and militancy that tenants produce for each other. The garden had long been tended as a shared resource. But after their association formed, it also became the physical location of their weekly meetings, a beachhead for building solidarity. "Plants Vs. Landlords," one protest flier proclaimed.[31] The threat of poor and working-class tenants is that the seeds of their organizing have taken root. As Botz once put it in disbelief, "We learned that the tenants really had no intention of ever leaving. They wanted to stay there for life."[32]

Hillside Villa has responded to the unwillingness of the city to intervene on their behalf by strengthening their relationships with other tenants in the LA Tenants Union. In May 2023, members of five local LATU chapters gathered at the building. The group split across the building's three entrances as perimeter guards, breaking off small contingents for medics and media. One group placed themselves across the staircase, some seated and some standing, filling in the gaps with their bodies. One packed a covered vestibule, shoulder to shoulder. One formed a line in front of the entrance, linked their arms, and knit themselves together to close the space between them. They bent their knees, braced for the attack. This time, the eviction blockade was just practice, but they knew it might not always be so.

HILLSIDE VILLA REVEALS the contradictions of a government run on real estate. In insisting that their claim to their housing is more legitimate than their landlord's, the tenants have opened the city to a crisis of legitimacy. Reliance on privately owned, publicly subsidized housing has sentenced these tenants to displacement; if the city wanted to protect affordable housing as an ideal and not a technicality, it would have to take the building away from its private owner. In trying to force a state purchase through eminent domain, Hillside Villa offers a model for affordable housing tenants across the country. But without a larger tenant movement, they may become an exception that proves the landlord's rule. Indeed, a proliferation of their strategy would generate a budgetary crisis too. Nationwide, almost a half a million affordable housing covenants will expire in the next eight years, including almost ten thousand in Los Angeles—that's twenty-five thousand tenants at risk of displacement in our city.[33] Perhaps one of Botz's lawyers framed it best: "There are covenants expiring throughout the city. You can't take all of them."[34]

Hillside Villa points toward a responsive, transformed state: budgets retracted from developer handouts, buildings put back into tenant control, the overturning of affordable housing policy, which works to inflate rents, displace poor and working-class people, to enrich private landlords. At the same time, the tenants show us how new kinds of housing governance can emerge from the ashes of the old—through occupations of privately owned space that shift the political, legal, and economic ground under the places we live in now.

The landlord has refused to let the city's appraisers onto the property. At the time of this writing, the city is still waiting for a court order to get inside; it can't appropriate the funds to purchase the building until the building has a price.[35] Meanwhile, Botz has filed thirty-five evictions.[36] The first group of tenants are on their way to court. But in August 2023, the Hillside Villa tenants association gathered in their shared garden once again. Surrounded by food, friends, and union siblings, they started a fire and drew close to the flames. One by one, they threw in their eviction notices and set them ablaze.

Carceral Housing: Echo Park Rise Up

Gustavo Otzoy was locked up twice in his life. Both times he was freed, he traveled to Echo Park Lake. When he first laid eyes on the park—sixteen acres of grass, paths, and palm trees, an expansive body of water, a pristine view of the downtown skyline—he'd just been released from immigrant detention. Forty years later, in June 2020, after serving a yearlong sentence in prison, he steered his bicycle toward the park again. He found it facelifted but familiar. He encountered a cluster of tents on the northwest corner of the park and asked someone if it was okay for him to stay. He'd never been homeless before.

Otzoy encountered a community organizing to meet its own needs.[37] They had access to the park's public bathrooms, soap, and drinking fountains, as well as the park itself. And since September 2019, residents had begun to build up their own infrastructure, which came to include a shared living room with seating sourced from the street, a pantry and kitchen with portable propane stoves, hand-built showers, and a community garden, where residents tended to vegetables and medicinal plants. That infrastructure would take a militarized sweep—seven hundred officers deployed over two days, more than $2 million of city funds, 182 arrests, and at least a dozen injuries—to destroy.[38]

As study after study affirms, unhoused tenants are pushed out of housing not due to an individual failing or character defect, but because of the cost of rent.[39] By 2023, the Los Angeles Homeless Services Authority would count 75,518 unhoused tenants, an increase of more than 50 percent in just seven years.[40] But rather than address the crisis with public housing, or prevent more tenants from losing their homes, city, state, and federal policy have funneled resources into sweeps and temporary shelter—to solve the problem of homelessness not with housing, but with banishment, criminalization, and warehousing. Unhoused tenants bear the brunt of the city's police force: though about one in ninety residents are unhoused, every one in six arrests and one in three reported police "uses of force" is of or against an unhoused person.[41]

IN THE FALL of 2019, park rangers and the LAPD made a point of targeting the people living at Echo Park Lake—issuing bogus tickets, making arrests on charges later quickly dismissed, and disrupting sleep. As one resident told UCLA's After Echo Park Research collective, police harassment at the park "was like a form of psychological torture. I would just finally be falling asleep, which is really hard to do as a woman sleeping outdoors sometimes, and then I would wake up to a group of men with guns banging on my tent telling me I couldn't be there. It was the middle of the night. I don't know where they expected me to go."[42]

Move-along orders and police sweeps separate unhoused tenants from what few supplies they've gathered to survive outdoors, including crucial documents, medications, and clothes they need to protect themselves from the elements. One of the first residents of the park, Ayman Ahmed, described the destabilization of sweeps as "having to rebuild a sense of house and a bed" over and over again.[43]

The tenants of Echo Park Lake decided to defend their encampment and stay put. In January 2020, they joined with housed supporters to form a human shield, blocking park rangers from tearing down tents. "This is not a cleanup," one insisted at the time, "This is a homeless eviction."[44] They wrote to their city councilmember as his "constituents," pleading not to be displaced from the support systems they'd built: "We hope you understand what this lake means to us—this has become our home in what is one of the darkest times of most of our lives."[45]

Pushing back against eviction united the group. They adopted a name: Echo Park Rise Up. Over the winter, they defended themselves from eviction at least four more times. In February 2020, in anticipation of a sweep, housed tenants set up tents alongside their unhoused neighbors, spending the night together. Rangers were forced to relent. As COVID-19 sent more and more tenants into the streets, the community at Echo Park Lake—and its militancy—grew.

Many of the tenants of Echo Park Lake were already connected to LA's homeless services agency. They had done everything their caseworkers asked: collected documents, signed paperwork. They were told to survive outside and wait.[46] But with no permanent housing available, they knew what was at the end of many of the city's waitlists: a bed in a congregate shelter, whose cramped, shared spaces were infamous for noxious conditions and COVID outbreaks; an unshaded tent in a fenced "safe sleep site," subject to twenty-four-hour surveillance; a "tiny home," where two residents share a prefabricated shed smaller than the American Correctional Association's standard prison cell for one.[47] The converted hotel rooms in Project Roomkey, an emergency pandemic program, banned guests, pets, or more than sixty gallons— one trash bag's worth—of personal belongings. Residents couldn't gather or visit each other and had to abide by a 7:00 p.m. curfew, after which they were locked inside. To many, those options didn't look like housing as the provision of a human need; they looked like incarceration for the crime of not being able to afford rent.

THE PANDEMIC HAD prompted the Centers for Disease Control and Prevention to issue an unprecedented recommendation: allow unhoused people to remain wherever they are.[48] Without recurring move-along orders or forced displacement, residents of the park enjoyed a rare taste of stability and the freedom that comes from being left alone. In May 2020, as the virus made access to basic hygiene even more crucial, unhoused residents and housed supporters blocked rangers from locking the park's bathrooms at night.[49] They won twenty-four-hour access. In collaboration with activists from Street Watch and Ground Game LA, the encampment coordinated weekly cell-phone charging for residents, whose access to electricity had been curtailed by pandemic closures of libraries and restaurants. Otzoy started to collect and distribute donations for the community: money, water, food, hygiene kits, and brand-new tents for people like him, who arrived at the park without anywhere else to go. He moved his tent next to the communal pantry and stored the precious tools he used for plumbing gigs inside.

Under the CDC's moratorium on sweeps, Ahmed said, tenants at Echo Park Lake experienced "more peace than they'd known in years."[50] As they organized to provide for their present survival needs, they could begin to imagine a future. Indeed, unhoused people's daily lives are a practice of occupation. They have no choice but to claim space to make their homes, often alongside others and necessarily in public space. Echo Park Rise Up imagined the park as a place not just to survive, but to thrive. That dream took concrete forms: a garden and kitchen, democratic processes for distributing resources, their own social alternative for housing the poor.

BUT THE PRESENCE of unhoused people challenged the park's function as an amenity, that is, a selling point for Echo Park. In 2013, the city had directed a mass of public resources to drawing in new residents and real estate speculation to the neighborhood, including a $45 million renovation of the park itself, as well as a gang injunction, which increased area police budgets—and police powers of discretion.[51] Gentrifying the historically working-class, immigrant community—a process often euphemized as "cleaning up" a neighborhood—was part of the citywide vision for economic development, centered on displacement and replacement: luring richer residents to expand its tax base and boost consumption, while underwriting the growth of land and property values. In a single decade, Echo Park had seen a doubling of home prices, which new owners and officials were keen to defend.

Multiple park residents had been raised in Echo Park yet, despite maintaining jobs, were unable to remain indoors—counting themselves among the two thousand people who become homeless in the city for every 5 percent rise in property values.[52] From the perspective of these residents, Echo Park had not been improved by the city's infusion of capital and cops; it had been removed. Almost a third of Echo Park's immigrant population was pushed out between 2000 and 2014.[53] Brenda, a resident who'd spent most of her sixty-two years within a few square miles of Echo Park Lake, said the encampment was the closest thing to her old community she'd experienced since having to live outside.[54]

In February 2020, a resentful coalition of home- and business owners circulated a petition on social media accusing the unhoused residents of "destroying" Echo Park: the petition claimed that the presence of an encampment prevented them from using the park and constituted a threat to their safety.[55] They called on the city to prevent the neighborhood from "becoming Skid Row." Consistent media coverage gave voice to this constituency as "stakeholders" of the park.[56] Then-councilmember Mitch O'Farrell encouraged them. As Ahmed put it, the encampment's detractors didn't see the "common humanity" between housed and unhoused people. Looking at the encampment's infrastructure, they saw not "a kitchen for people who are trying to cook who have nowhere to cook. They [saw] dirty people [whom] they don't count the same as them, making their area dirty."

Aligned with property values rather than human rights, city agencies conspired against residents of Echo Park Lake by denying or removing services. As public-records requests revealed, Chief Park Ranger Joe Losorelli had helped deny the park access to a hygiene trailer with showers, lest it become "another Occupy LA."[57] Sanitation ceased to collect trash from the area around the encampment. The Parks Department cut off electricity only from the lights around their tents. Then the lack of sanitation and lighting was leveraged as justification for a future sweep. The city refused to provide harm reduction and medical services to the community, then deployed overdose deaths at the park to call for the encampment's removal.[58] As in "constructive evictions" that drive tenants out of their homes with uninhabitable conditions, the city acted as slumlord, speculator, and sheriff.

AT THE LAKE, residents had the autonomy to come and go, to remain with their partners and pets, to cook for themselves, and to analyze and address their needs themselves. At weekly meetings, they gathered to make collective decisions about distributing their resources and defending their space. "We all got involved in working together there, to make the kitchen, clean the bathrooms," Otzoy said. "We were like a family."[59] Echo Park Lake was a place "where one could leave one's tent and move around in the world knowing it would still be there later," one resident told UCLA researchers.[60] "No one went hungry," said another.[61] By summer 2020, the group announced on social media that they'd initiated a jobs program, paying residents $10 an hour for roles including "park security, shower monitor, donation inventory, donation tent distribution, police and community liaisons."[62] When George Floyd's murder sent the largest protest movement in US history into the streets of Los Angeles, hundreds gathered at Echo Park Lake to connect the racism of policing to the racism of real estate, which produces disproportionate rates of homelessness among Black people.

There were three basic rules at the encampment: don't steal from other residents; keep your area clean; and if you're going to use drugs, do so inside your tent. It wasn't always perfect. Interpersonal conflict took place in the theater of public space. Many residents were sober, others were not. ("If you don't give people stability,"

Ahmed said, "that hit becomes their stability . . . it's consistent."[63])
Working through large-scale social crises like the opioid epidemic,
the group held conflict-resolution and harm-reduction trainings.[64]
They collected sharps and distributed Narcan (a medication that
treats opioid overdoses) as well as clean needles. As a banner hang-
ing across two tents at the north edge of the park read, "Healing
happens here."

Over time, the coordination of resources became an offensive
as well as defensive practice for the group. "When the mayor cut
funding for showers during COVID-19, we didn't just accept it, we
built our own showers," they announced on a fundraising page.[65]
"When the city decided to then cut our water supply we didn't just
accept it, we rallied community support and now have full gallons
every day." As Ahmed summarized about organizing in the context of state abandonment, "You don't ask permission from the city,
when they don't care." One night, residents and organizers strung
up their own battery- and solar-powered lights. They planted a veg-
etable garden as an independent source of food.

"We were figuring out how to solve these problems that come
about due to the lack of affordable housing in California," resident
Cecelia Acho told the *Los Angeles Downtown News*.[66] By claiming
territory, building community, collectivizing resources, and organizing to change their conditions, Echo Park Lake Rise Up posed
their own solution to the crisis of homelessness: reappropriat-
ing space for collective survival. As Leilani Farha, former United
Nations special rapporteur on adequate housing put it, Echo Park
revealed "homeless encampments as human rights claims."[67] This
was public space not as a civilizing resource for the masses, not
as an amenity to be marketed by speculators to increase land and
property values, but as a seedbed for collective sovereignty. The

encampment was an occupation: against the interests of the real estate state, which had both pushed tenants outside and sought to sweep them from view, it addressed the social need for housing by claiming space to live.

IN THE WINTER of 2021, police stepped up their presence, as did nonprofit and city workers with offers of temporary housing. Officials promised that every resident of the park would be placed somewhere indoors. Residents were circumspect. Tied to the threat of eviction and the presence of police, what the city called "offers" were mostly orders: ultimatums made at gunpoint, a choice between acceptance and banishment, compliance or arrest. Promises of "housing" would provide the legal and rhetorical cover for police to purge them from public space. And those temporary, carceral spaces were less "housing" than arms of the prison system. As one protest sign summarized, "Housing without autonomy is internment." Even to enter temporary housing, unhoused people have to give up their rights. They sign a contract as a "participant" and must testify that "no tenancy is created."⁶⁸ "You're in their hands," Otzoy said. "They can do with you what they want."⁶⁹

By the end of March 2021, city officials suggested that the city would close the park for repairs. Residents recognized that a final sweep was imminent. On March 23, the encampment put out a call on social media for support. "We've had nothing but each other this year and honestly it's been a relief," they wrote. "Without the constant LAPD and city harassment uprooting our lives we've been able to grow. . . . Our demand is simply this: please continue to leave us alone, or stand with us."⁷⁰ The next morning, Ahmed spoke to nearly five hundred people who'd gathered to defend their right to remain. He summarized the power of the occupation and the threat that it posed: "What we're building here is not a tent city. It is a blueprint for how poor people will organize. It is a plan for empowerment."

On March 24, at least four hundred cops in riot gear faced down the remaining members of the encampment and their supporters. The mass of protestors made a spectacle of a routine practice: the police were called to sweep an encampment where unhoused people were attempting to make a home. Strategizing around the community kitchen, residents and supporters asked each other in disbelief, "What was so terrifying about a hundred people living in the park that the city needed a military operation to get rid of us?" Ahmed responded in a whisper, "We got CCS here. It's a secret weapon." Then he broke out in a smile: "Cute Community Shit."

Officers wielded batons, launched foam bullets at point-blank range, and tackled members of the crowd. One officer's swinging nightstick broke a journalist's arm.[71] By morning, the last of the residents awoke to find themselves completely fenced inside the park with a mile-long, chain-link enclosure. In an Instagram live stream, they compared their surroundings to an open-air prison.[72] The councilmember celebrated the mass eviction as "the single largest housing event in the history of the city."[73] A year later, the fallout of the event would become clear: only 7 percent of residents had been placed in permanent housing. Half were missing. Nine had died.

As outlined in LAPD's 101-page "After Action Report," installing the fence was the central mission of police action."[74] Their strategy was to establish and guard an enclosure. The report describes the unhoused residents of the park as "an organized and well-equipped group of people experiencing homelessness [who] took control of the northwest corner of Echo Park." It highlights solidar-

ity, the tenants' "unusual level of external support with easy access
to resources like food, camping equipment, and electronics." The
police recognized the threat as a contest of ownership over territory
they needed to defend by force. "As the Echo Park encampment
grew," the report described, "so did the activists' claims of ownership over the public space."[75] The fence remained around the park
for over two years.

A FEW WEEKS after the eviction, Otzoy gathered with several former residents of Echo Park Lake at Pershing Square—a shadeless,
nearly benchless park, redesigned in 1994 to harden its architecture against unhoused people. They commiserated over the pain of
losing the support of the park and shared their resolve to continue
the struggle. "Fighting this injustice helps me to get out the pain
that I have," Otzoy emphasized later. "It helps me."[76] The group
founded Unhoused Tenants Against Carceral Housing (UTACH),
a tenants association for unhoused people within the temporary
housing system and out on the streets. In a year of organizing,
they succeeded in shrinking lock-in hours at housing sites, establishing access to Narcan, and preventing mass evictions as the city
aimed to shutter Project Roomkey sites. Now, some of UTACH's
members have folded into LATU. Otzoy, who managed to secure
a voucher, joined the Union de Vecinos Eastside Local. Their presence in the union reminds us to recognize unhoused people as key
political subjects in the struggle for housing liberation for all.

Deprived of homes by the capitalist housing system designed
around the interests of real estate speculators, developers, and landlords, rather than the needs of tenants, the residents of Echo Park
Lake claimed their right to build community, to take up space, to

continue to exist in a city bent on their expulsion or containment. Their occupation of the park served as both a means of self-defense, protecting unhoused tenants from police harassment and incarceration, and an experiment in an alternative housing, grounded in collective self-organization. The growing solidarity between housed and unhoused people promised a movement of tenants cohered under a shared politics, beyond differences that hold us apart. "To create our own justice," Otzoy said at the time, "that's what we're doing right now."[77]

Occupying Our Homes

It's much easier to name all the ways that rent harms us than it is to imagine a future without it—or figure out how we get from here to there. In the tradition of liberation theology, a prophet has a dual function: to denounce the present system and to announce another kind of life. In our nascent movement, our actions are experimental and provisional, yet they share this double character: a refusal of the profit motive as mediator of all social relations, and a promise that another way of arranging ourselves, our housing, and our cities is possible.

None of our struggles have brought us close to our ideal. We know even our unqualified victories can be rolled back. Still, the partial character of our fights and campaigns, waged by neighbors desperate to stay in their neighborhood, a building fed up with harassment, tenants who simply can't afford rent, can guide us to a new horizon. Reflected in the everyday activity of poor and working-class tenants, that horizon comes into view: individual ownership transformed into collective stewardship.

For us, this process is alive, if implicit, in every rent strike, union meeting, and occupation of public and common space. A fight might begin with one neighbor catching another in the hallway, discovering the power of coming together as a building. Often their campaigns require the support of a larger organization, a union, which can offer them resources, guide them, and help coordinate them at the scale of a block or neighborhood. Most spectacular are those struggles that confront the state in its effort to violently displace those who cannot pay. But at each moment of its development, our work discloses something about the tenant movement, a hymn that can be read off every page: that the stake of our struggle is nothing less than the land itself, and the shape of the lives we can lead on it.

In the examples above, tenants fight back against affordable housing on the one hand and carceral housing on the other, those policies for housed and unhoused tenants that prop up and perpetuate the real estate regime. As Hillside Villa shows, our movement must both invest in tenants associations to defend our housing and make demands of the state that produce budgetary and legitimacy crises. These open the door for real representation—tenant enfranchisement—while they expand independent tenant power. Rather than just demand new social housing, Hillside Villa suggests, we must socialize housing.[78] At the same time, as Echo Park shows, we can reclaim space for ourselves directly, building autonomous capacity in opposition to the state's. Echo Park Rise Up took for granted that land is a social good that belongs to all people and acted accordingly, defending their community and its infrastructure.

Both by making demands of the state and by building an alternative to it, tenants build power to retask its instruments of redistribution and dismantle its tools of repression. In contests

over land use and land management—that is, land governance—
we contest state sovereignty.

TO SOCIAL AND political demands, the state answers with technical and economic processes that only facilitate capitalist accumulation. Under this paradigm, the call for public housing is answered
with privatization schemes. The call for community investment
is answered with gentrification. The call to solve the housing crisis is answered with affordable and carceral housing. The actions
of tenants in struggle point to the direction we can follow to overcome these contradictions. Just as tree roots slowly break up the
sidewalks that order the spaces where we live, we can cultivate our
movement over time, through the patient, everyday activity of organizing, which Ella Baker called "spadework."

The tenant as a political category collects the landless and propertyless, the disenfranchised and undocumented, those *placed* outside the category of citizen, even outside of the category of human.
To reclaim a place is to struggle for, with, alongside, and because
some of us are made to be "out of place" by the logic of policing and
property. By deepening relationships with our neighbors, we can
resist displacement and build lasting institutions of tenant democracy. We fight dispossession not with possession but by cultivating
new forms of belonging.

The abolition of rent is the absence of landlords and real estate
speculators and the presence of new relationships to each other and
to places where we live. Abolition is antagonistic and prefigurative,
a creative and a destructive process. As we reclaim our housing, we
stop landlords from stealing our wages. As we reclaim the territory
of the city, we block speculators from reaping the benefits of our

collective labor. The struggle against rent is a struggle for collective control over territory and our resources, such that all housing becomes social housing. This is a utopian vision in which housing can be claimed as much as built, where self-organization can flourish, and where we can begin, by organizing and *occupying* our buildings and blocks, to bring the world of our imaginings into the one that exists now.

"I joined because I liked it," Isabel Garcia told us of the Second Street Tenants Association. "Me gustaba. Platicar. Convivir."[79] *Convivir* literally means to live or coexist with, to be around, but a fuller translation includes multiple registers: to get together, to live together, to hang out, to spend time together, to get along, and to get close to. Spanish speakers often complain that *convivir* is untranslatable; like a picture, it would take a thousand English words.

The sense of connection was the glue that held the Second Street Tenants Association together, giving Garcia strength to endure the landlord's campaign of harassment, even to take a risk in solidarity with her neighbors during the height of the pandemic, when some of her neighbors couldn't pay rent at all. "If they're doing this, support them," she thought. "If they're gonna kick one of you out, they're gonna kick everybody out."[80] Of course, it was a risk to go on rent strike, yet the association helped her understand that it was also a risk not to try.

In the context of so much uncertainty in the early pandemic months, of lockdowns, lost work, and sickness, how could they hand over what little they had to a landlord? "If we give our money to the landlord it's gone," Anne Orchier summarized. "The guarantee is that [our landlord] doesn't bother us for one month."[81] The association found solace in the union's frame around the strike: Food Not Rent. As Yesenia put it, tenants had two choices: "You pay rent or you eat."

The association allowed its members to *descargar*, meaning to unburden themselves, Garcia said. "We have this movement so we can talk, to let things out, to say what you feel, to talk about what you're going through and even the things that you didn't go through."[82] Defeating the shame wrought by isolation, the group calculated the rent debt they accrued on the strike, wielding it as collective leverage and undermining the landlord's claims that he lacked funds for necessary repairs. The tenants got their own estimates for what it would cost to fix a fence that threatened to tip onto their building and to ground a shaky staircase to the building's second floor. Using the rent they'd kept, they realized, they would be able to afford to pay for that and then some. In some ways, withholding rent had made them more, rather than less, secure.

After the landlord's attack on their garden, some members of the association and the broader union joined together early on a Friday morning to set things right. They restored their gathering space, replanting the spiked and poisonous plants into neat rows along the side of the yard, out of the reach of children and pets, returning access to their trash bins and the fruit of their trees. As rushed and shoddy a job as the landlord had done, the group was careful not to destroy his property. They repurposed the wood into a trellis, where jasmine would soon grow. On a break, the group partook in the ritual of Epiphany Day: within a sweet, circular loaf of bread, a miniature statue of baby Jesus is hidden; whoever finds that piece is responsible for feeding the group at their next gathering, held on día de la Candelaria. At the end of the day, they put up a hand-painted sign, christening "Isabel's Garden."

The Second Street Tenants Association's commitment has been demonstrated in a series of escalations that have drawn more people into their fight. When the landlord installed surveillance cameras over their common spaces and in their hallways—emailing them pictures of their comings and goings—the association hosted a party for their block. They blew up balloons, strategically placing them in front of each camera's line of sight. When the landlord filed eviction notices for rent strikers, they hosted another party, this time for the Autonomous Tenants Union Network's first in-person convention. They blocked the street with roadwork barricades borrowed from around the neighborhood. In place of passing cars, they set up a PA to play cumbia, an enormous pot of homemade mole, and a cake to celebrate movement elder Walt Senterfitt's seventy-fifth birthday.

In fall of 2023, the landlord put the building back up for sale, at $1,999,000, nearly four times what he had paid for it just eleven years before. Second Street is now researching financial instruments to buy their building as a cooperative. Their goal is not just to stabilize their building, but to stabilize the movement's presence in their neighborhood.

During an attempt at mediation, the landlord told the city attorney's office that he'd drop his tenants' evictions provided they stop their events. He said the tenants association's movie nights, chapter meetings, and food distribution were as threatening to him as eviction notices. Those communal gatherings are not outwardly aggressive actions, but, in a way, he is right: taking away his ability to turn their neighbors against them, building support for emergency response, those actions grow the power of tenants.

WHEN WE ASKED Garcia what it might be like if she and her neighbors no longer had to worry about rent, or about having a landlord, she replied, "All the tenants could live together, come together, engage and interact with each other."[83] The word she used, again, was *convivir*. The means and ends of the tenants movement are one and the same: we get together, live together, hang out, spend time, get along, and get close to each other. The tenant movement is a concrete project to bring about another way of life.

The loquat and avocado trees that Garcia planted in her yard as a teenager have grown to shade a movement that also grows. They now tower over the structure of the house, guarding a community of neighbors, an organization of tenants, and the faith to continue through every victory and every defeat. Looking up at them from the garden, we're reminded of the spiritual we often sing, which prefigures the power we want: collective control over where and how we live; a right to housing that encompasses a right to survive, a right to take up space, a right to migrate, and a right to stay put. "Like a tree planted by the water," the song goes, "we shall not be moved."

ACKNOWLEDGMENTS

WE THANK EACH and every member of the LA Tenants Union, past, present, and future. Your actions give meaning to anything we could write. We are especially grateful to everyone who took the time to be interviewed for this project. We also thank each member of School of Echoes, for a near decade of shared analysis and strategy, including Dont Rhine, Elizabeth Blaney, and Walt Senterfitt, whose decades of experience in disparate movements from SNCC to ACT UP flow together into the union we helped start. We were more than lucky to have a comrade, Ben Mabie, for an editor, and thank him for his stewardship and guidance, as well as Katy O'Donnell, Charlotte Heltai, and the whole team at Haymarket, for turning publishing into building community.

No one with their name not on the cover had more to do with the shape of this book than Rose Lenehan. We owe a special debt to Alexander Ferrer, Anne Orchier, Annie Powers, David Anthony Albright, David Madden, Marques Vestal, Justin Gilmore, and Sam Stein, who generously contributed their expertise and insight to chapter drafts, and to Brendan O'Connor, for ordering our mess of citations. We drew continual inspiration from spaces convened by Ananya Roy and thank all of our collaborators in the Institute on Inequality and Democracy and the Housing the Third Reconstruction Freedom School.

Tracy would especially like to thank the people who made the work of writing possible. I would be capable of very little without Emily Gaines Tecchio. You are gravity. Rose Lenehan organized me. My oldest friend, Martha Tenney, shared institutional library access through ceaseless push notifications. Dearest Mara Mckevitt deliberated for hours on the phone. Jamie Lauren Keiles believed it was possible when I did not. I would also like to thank Emily Cooke and Katie McDonough, who edited the texts at the *New Republic* from which some of the language and research in this work were drawn; Canal Street Research, Center for Research in the Humanities at the New York Public Library, and Center for Fiction for quiet spaces; the members of the James Boggs Reading Group and RATS NYC; and my family. Finally, my own tenants association managed to turn the roller coaster of our rent strike—sixteen months and counting—into the stability I needed to write this book.

Leonardo would especially like to thank the members of Union de Vecinos; the East Side Local of LA Tenants Union; the women of Pico Aliso: Carmen Mendoza, Manuela Lomeli, Gaby Castillo, Maria Ramirez (Chayo), Laura Zelaya, Laura Serrano, Delmira Gonzalez, Ana Hernandez, Bun Bun Hurd, Yolanda Gallo, Lety Zepeda, Maria Torres; the men of Pico Aliso: Walter Mendoza, Raul Serrano, Ruben Gonzalez; and El Comite de los 36, who guided and led the construction of something new. Kenia Alcocer, Laura Cuadros, Elizabeth Blaney, Elsa Casillas, Ofelia Platon, Blanca Espinoza, and Juan Hernandez changed their lives to build Union de Vecinos. I could not forget Gilda Haas, Jackie Leavitt, David Etezadi, Elena Popp, Dont Rhine, Walt Senterfitt, and Robert Sember. Finally, Teresa, Arantza, and Leonardo, my family, who have endured the consequences of my organizing work, because there is no text without struggle, and there is no struggle without love.

NOTES

Introduction

1. Mike Davis, *City of Quartz: Excavating the Future in Los Angeles* (London and New York: Verso, 2018).

2. Kelly Lytle Hernández, *City of Inmates: Conquest, Rebellion, and the Rise of Human Caging in Los Angeles, 1771–1965*. Justice, Power, and Politics (Chapel Hill: University of North Carolina Press, 2017).

3. Gwynedd Stuart, "The 'World's Most Expensive Home' Has Been Unveiled and It's Really Something," *Los Angeles Magazine*, January 13, 2021, https://lamag.com/featured/most-expensive-home-the-one-bel-air; Lexis-Olivier Ray, "In Sunny Los Angeles, More Homeless People Die from the Cold than in SF and NYC, Combined," *L.A. Taco*, January 19, 2021, https://lataco.com/homeless-la-death-hypothermia.

4. Michele Lerner, "Did Your House Earn More than You Did in 2021?," *Washington Post*, April 4, 2022, https://www.washingtonpost.com/business/2022/04/06/did-your-house-earn-more-than-you-did-2021/.

Chapter 1: Rent Is the Crisis

1. Nicole Bachaud, "Three Roommates of Four Jobs Needed to Afford a Two-Bedroom Rental on Minimum Wage," Zillow, January 31, 2023, https://www.zillow.com/research/minimum-wage-rent-32060.

2. "Spending 30% of Income on Rent Is the New Normal in Many US Metros," Moody's Analytics, May 16, 2023, https://www.moodys.com/web/en/us/about/insights/data-stories/us-rental-housing-affordability.html.

3. Daniel Flaming, Patrick Burns, and Jane Carlen, "Escape Routes: Meta-Analysis of Homelessness in L.A.," Economic Roundtable, April 24, 2018, https://economicrt.org/publication/escape-routes/.

4. Kevin Freking, "US Homelessness up 12% to Highest Reported Level as Rents Soar and Coronavirus Pandemic Aid Lapses," Associated Press, December 15, 2023, https://apnews.com/article/homelessness-increase-rent-hud-covid-60bd88687e1aef1b02d25425798bd3b1.

5. Juan Pablo Garnham, Carl Gershenson, and Matthew Desmond, "New Data Release Shows That 3.6 Million Eviction Cases Were Filed in the United States in 2018," *Eviction Lab* (blog), July 11, 2022, https://eviction-lab.org/new-eviction-data-2022/.

6. "U.S. Renters Spent $4.5 Trillion on Housing This Decade," *Zillow Media-Room* (blog), December 12, 2019, https://zillow.mediaroom.com/2019-12-12-U-S-Renters-Spent-4-5-Trillion-on-Housing-This-Decade.

7. Kevin Schaul and Jonathan O'Connell, "Investors Bought up a Record Share of Homes Last Year," *Washington Post*, February 16, 2022, https://www.washingtonpost.com/business/interactive/2022/housing-market-in-vestors/; Elena Botella, "Investment Firms Aren't Buying All the Houses. But They Are Buying the Most Important Ones," *Slate*, June 19, 2021, https://slate.com/business/2021/06/blackrock-invitation-houses-invest-ment-firms-real-estate.html; Francesca Mari, "Imagine a Renters' Utopia. It Might Look Like Vienna," *New York Times*, May 23, 2023, https://www.nytimes.com/2023/05/23/magazine/vienna-social-housing.html.

8. Frances Fox Piven and Richard Cloward, *Poor People's Movements: Why They Succeed, How They Fail* (New York: Knopf Doubleday Publishing Group, 1979), 2.

9. In a technical sense, the word *rent* refers to any income derived solely from owning and controlling an asset. Paradigmatic is land, for which rent is an entitlement derived from monopolizing slices of the earth. But a utility company also extracts rent by controlling access to the infra-structure systems for electricity or gas. Rents can even be claimed on intellectual property, like when a company issues an exclusive patent on a life-saving drug. When we talk about "rent" in this book, we mean it in the same way most everyday people do: the monthly handover of our income to the people or corporations who own our homes. See: Alexander Ferrer, "Why We Should Be Arguing about Rent," *Progressive City*, December 22, 2020, https://www.progressivecity.net/single-post/why-we-should-be-arguing-about-rent.

10. Alicia Mazzara, "Rents Have Risen More than Incomes in Nearly Every State since 2001," *Off the Charts* (blog), December 10, 2019, https://www.

cbpp.org/blog/rents-have-risen-more-than-incomes-in-nearly-every-state-since-2001#; Drew Desilver, "For Most U.S. Workers, Real Wages Have Barely Budged in Decades," *Pew Research Center* (blog), August 7, 2018, https://www.pewresearch.org/short-reads/2018/08/07/for-most-us-workers-real-wages-have-barely-budged-for-decades/.

11.   Sophia Wedeen, "Greater Assistance Needed to Combat the Persistence of Substandard Housing," *Housing Perspectives* (blog), August 1, 2023, https://www.jchs.harvard.edu/blog/greater-assistance-needed-combat-persistence-substandard-housing; Alexia Fernández Campbell, "Gas Leaks, Mold, and Rats: Millions of Americans Live in Hazardous Homes," *Atlantic*, July 25, 2016, https://www.theatlantic.com/business/archive/2016/07/gas-leaks-mold-and-rats-millions-of-americans-live-in-hazardous-homes/492689/.

12.   "America's Rental Housing 2022," Joint Center for Housing Studies of Harvard University, 2022.

13.   Sammi Aibinder and Lindsay Owens, "No Room for Rent: Addressing Rising Rent Prices through Public Investment and Public Power," Roosevelt Institute, November 2021, https://rooseveltinstitute.org/wp-content/uploads/2021/11/RI_NoRoomForRentAddressingRisingRentPrices_IssueBrief_202110.pdf.

14.   "One part of society thus exacts tribute from another for the permission to inhabit the earth, as landed property in general assigns the landlord the privilege of exploiting the terrestrial body, the bowels of the earth, the air, and thereby the maintenance and development of life." Karl Marx, *Capital: A Critique of Political Economy*, vol. 3, trans. David Fernbach (London; New York: Penguin Classics, 1993), 908–9. See also Robert Nichols, *Theft Is Property!: Dispossession and Critical Theory* (Durham: Duke University Press, 2020), https://doi.org/10.2307/j.ctv11smqjz.

15.   Drew DeSilver, "As National Eviction Ban Expires, a Look at Who Rents and Who Owns in the U.S.," *Pew Research Center* (blog), https://www.pewresearch.org/short-reads/2021/08/02/as-national-eviction-ban-expires-a-look-at-who-rents-and-who-owns-in-the-u-s/.

16.   Peter J. Mateyka and Jayne Yoo, "Share of Income Needed to Pay Rent Increased the Most for Low-Income Households from 2019 to 2021," *Census.Gov* (blog), March 2, 2023, https://www.census.gov/library/stories/2023/03/low-income-renters-spent-larger-share-of-income-on-rent.html. Also see David Harvey, "Class-Monopoly Rent, Finance Capital and

the Urban Revolution," in *Readings in Urban Analysis*, ed. Robert W. Lake, 1st ed. (Abingdon and New York: Routledge, 2017), 250–77, https://doi.org/10.4324/9781315128061-15.

17. US Census Bureau, "Rental Housing Finance Survey (RHFS)," United States Census Bureau, July 21, 2022, https://www.census.gov/programs-surveys/rhfs.html.

18. See Erik Swyngedouw et al., "'Value Grabbing': A Political Ecology of Rent," *Capitalism, Nature, Socialism* 28, no. 3 (2017): 28–47, https://doi.org/10.1080/10455752.2016.1278027.

19. Josh Ryan-Collins, Toby Lloyd, and Laurie Macfarlane, *Rethinking the Economics of Land and Housing* (London: Zed Books, 2023), https://www.bloomsbury.com/us/rethinking-the-economics-of-land-and-housing-9781350374270/. See also George Monbiot et al., *Land for the Many: Changing the Way Our Fundamental Asset Is Used, Owned and Governed* (United Kingdom: Labour Party, 2019), https://landforthemany.uk/.

20. The expansion of mortgage credit, says the Organisation for Economic Co-operation and Development, has increased real house prices by at least 30 percent. See Josh Ryan-Collins, *Why Can't You Afford a Home?* (Cambridge, UK, and Medford, MA: Polity Press, 2019).

21. Tyler Wright (@DefiningWealth), "Bank Buys Me the House. Tenants Pay off the Loan. Property Manager Handles Everything. I Collect Cash Every Month. Inflation Builds Me Massive Wealth. Real Estate. 🏠," X (formerly Twitter), April 7, 2022, https://twitter.com/DefiningWealth/status/1512028106793570306.

22. Cyrus Vanover, "How Much Should I Charge for Rent: Guide to Setting Rental Rates," *BiggerPockets* (blog), September 21, 2023, https://www.biggerpockets.com/blog/how-much-to-charge-for-rent.

23. Billy Butcher, CEO of the KKR Real Estate Select Trust, told CNBC: "The depreciation from our properties has covered 100% of the income generated by our properties, and there's no tax on that dividend." Carlos Waters, "How Wall Street's REIT Giants Are Reshaping U.S. Real Estate," CNBC, September 1, 2023, https://www.cnbc.com/2023/09/01/how-wall-streets-reit-giants-are-reshaping-us-real-estate.html. See also Matt Levin, "Data Dig: Are Foreign Investors Driving up Real Estate in Your California Neighborhood?," CalMatters, March 7, 2018, https://calmatters.org/housing/2018/03/data-dig-are-foreign-investors-driving-up-real-estate-in-your-california-neighborhood/.

24. Celeste Hornbach et al., "Corporate Windfalls or Social Housing Conversions? The Looming Mortgage Crisis and the Choices Facing New York," Community Service Society, November 2020, https://smhttp-ssl-58547.nexcesscdn.net/nycss/images/uploads/pubs/Foreclosure_Report_V111.pdf.

25. For an elegant summation of the rent trap, see Sally Rooney, "Renters Are Being Exploited and Evictions Must Be Stopped," *Irish Times*, March 18, 2023, https://www.irishtimes.com/life-style/2023/03/18/sally-rooney-renters-are-being-exploited-and-evictions-must-be-stopped/.

26. Conor Dougherty and Ben Casselman, "When It's Easy to Be a Landlord, No One Wants to Sell," *New York Times*, February 11, 2023, https://www.nytimes.com/2023/02/11/business/economy/real-estate-market-landlords.html.

27. Charlie Dulik, "Pity the Landlord," *The Baffler*, October 2, 2023, https://thebaffler.com/latest/pity-the-landlord-dulik.

28. Patrick Clark, "Landlords Are Taking over the U.S. Housing Market," *Bloomberg*, February 23, 2017, https://www.bloomberg.com/news/articles/2017-02-23/landlords-are-taking-over-the-u-s-housing-market.

29. Anthony Cilluffo, A. W. Geiger, and Richard Fry, "More U.S. Households Are Renting than at Any Point in 50 Years," *Pew Research Center* (blog), July 19, 2017, https://www.pewresearch.org/short-reads/2017/07/19/more-u-s-households-are-renting-than-at-any-point-in-50-years/; Sophie Kasakove, "First-Time Home Buyers Are Getting Squeezed Out by Investors and Corporations," *New York Times*, April 23, 2022, https://www.nytimes.com/2022/04/23/us/corporate-real-estate-investors-housing-market.html.

30. In Los Angeles, the top 0.1 percent of all landlords now own more than 21 percent of rental housing, while the largest 1 percent owns more than 40 percent. Alexander Ferrer et al., "The Practice of Landlording: A Sectoral Analysis of Lessors of Residential Buildings and Dwellings Industry (NAICS 53111) in Los Angeles County and California," UCLA Luskin School of Public Affairs, Fall 2021.

31. Francesca Mari, "A $60 Billion Housing Grab by Wall Street," *New York Times*, March 4, 2020, https://www.nytimes.com/2020/03/04/magazine/wall-street-landlords.html.

32. Brett Christophers, *Our Lives in Their Portfolios: Why Asset Managers Own the World* (London and New York: Verso, 2023).

33. Elora Lee Raymond et al., "From Foreclosure to Eviction: Housing Insecurity in Corporate-Owned Single-Family Rentals," *Cityscape* 20, no. 3 (2018): 159–88; Maya Abood, *Wall Street Landlords Turn American Dream into a Nightmare*, ACCE Institute, Americans for Financial Reform, and Public Advocates Making Rights Real, January 2018, https://assets.nationbuilder.com/acceinstitute/pages/1153/attachments/original/1570049936/WallstreetLandlordsFinalReport.pdf.

34. Erik Gartland, "Hidden Housing Instability: 3.7 Million People Live in Doubled-Up Households," *Off the Charts* (blog), September 6, 2022, https://www.cbpp.org/blog/hidden-housing-instability-37-million-people-live-in-doubled-up-households.

35. Brittny Mejia et al., "How L.A. Became the Most Overcrowded Place in the U.S.," *Los Angeles Times*, October 19, 2022, https://www.latimes.com/california/story/2022-10-19/los-angeles-history-overcrowding-united-states.

36. Kris Billhardt, "Rapid Re-Housing: Considerations for Homeless Service Providers Supporting Families Impacted by Domestic Violence," Family Violence Prevention and Services Program, Family and Youth Services Bureau, U.S. Department of Health and Human Services, 2018, https://safehousingpartnerships.org/sites/default/files/2018-06/Key%20Considerations%20for%20RRH%20w%20Survivors.pdf.

37. Corianne Payton Scally and Dulce Gonzalez, "Renters Are More Likely than Homeowners to Struggle with Paying for Basic Needs | Urban Institute," *Urban Wire* (blog), November 1, 2018, https://www.urban.org/urban-wire/renters-are-more-likely-homeowners-struggle-paying-basic-needs.

38. Whitney Airgood-Obrycki, Alexander Hermann, and Sophia Wedeen, *The Rent Eats First: Rental Housing Unaffordability in the US*, Joint Center for Housing Studies of Harvard University, January 2021, https://www.jchs.harvard.edu/sites/default/files/research/files/harvard_jchs_rent_eats_first_airgood-obrycki_hermann_wedeen_2021.pdf.

39. Christophers, *Our Lives in Their Portfolios*, 57, 156.

40. Thomas Piketty offers a sanitized version of this as a definition of rent: "The increment of well-being due to sleeping and living under a roof rather than outside." Thomas Piketty, *Capital in the Twenty-First Century*, trans. Arthur Goldhammer (Cambridge, MA, and London: The Belknap Press of Harvard University Press, 2017), 213.

41. "Why Eviction Matters," Eviction Lab, 2018, https://evictionlab.org/why-eviction-matters/.

42. Stefanie DeLuca and Eva Rosen, "Housing Insecurity among the Poor Today," *Annual Review of Sociology* 48, no. 1 (2022): 343–71, https://doi.org/10.1146/annurev-soc-090921-040646.

43. "Eviction Notices (February–November 2023)," Kenneth Mejia, Los Angeles City Controller, December 2023, https://controller.lacity.gov/landings/evictions.

44. Sophie Beiers, Sandra Park, and Linda Morris, "Clearing the Record: How Eviction Sealing Laws Can Advance Housing Access for Women of Color," *American Civil Liberties Union* (blog), January 10, 2020, https://www.aclu.org/news/racial-justice/clearing-the-record-how-eviction-sealing-laws-can-advance-housing-access-for-women-of-color.

45. The complex language and procedures of our court system mean that to fight eviction we often need a lawyer's expertise. But while about 90 percent of landlords nationwide are represented by an attorney in eviction proceedings, only about 10 percent of tenants are. Most tenants can only hope to receive a lawyer through overwhelmed charities or chronically underfunded public programs. Sarah Holder, Kriston Capps, and Mackenzie Hawkins, "In Housing Court, a Scramble for Eviction-Fighting Lawyers," Bloomberg, April 27, 2023, https://www.bloomberg.com/news/features/2023-04-27/as-renters-struggle-eviction-busting-lawyers-are-in-short-supply.

46. Matt Bruenig, "Violence Vouchers: A Descriptive Account of Property," *Matt Bruenig Dot Com* (blog), March 28, 2014, https://mattbruenig.com/2014/03/28/violence-vouchers-a-descriptive-account-of-property/.

47. Even a public landlord relies on state violence to evict its residents.

48. David J. Madden and Peter Marcuse, *In Defense of Housing: The Politics of Crisis* (London and New York: Verso, 2016), 76.

49. The dynamics of real estate capture often turn tenants' own ingenuity into scripts for flips. See Sharon Zukin, *Loft Living: Culture and Capital in Urban Change*, 25th anniversary edition (New Brunswick, NJ: Rutgers University Press, 2014).

50. See Matthew Desmond, *Poverty, by America* (New York: Crown, 2023), 91.

51. Neil Bhutta et al., "Changes in U.S. Family Finances from 2016 to 2019: Evidence from the Survey of Consumer Finances," *Federal Reserve Bulletin* 106, no. 5 (September 2020).

52. We outline the history of racism in shaping housing markets and housing markets shaping racism in chapter 2. See also: Ida Danewid, "The Fire This

Time: Grenfell, Racial Capitalism and the Urbanisation of Empire," *European Journal of International Relations* 26, no. 1 (March 1, 2020): 289–313, https://doi.org/10.1177/1354066119858388; Brenna Bhandar and Alberto Toscano, "Race, Real Estate and Real Abstraction," *Radical Philosophy*, no. 194 (December 2015), https://www.radicalphilosophy.com/article/race-real-estate-and-real-abstraction; Benjamin F. Teresa, "The Reemergence of Land Contracts in Chicago: Racialized Class-Monopoly Rent as a Recursive Objective in Capitalist Property Markets," *Geoforum* 130 (March 2022): 35–45, https://doi.org/10.1016/j.geoforum.2022.02.004.

53.   Ellora Derenoncourt et al., "Wealth of Two Nations: The U.S. Racial Wealth Gap, 1860–2020," Working Paper, Working Paper Series, National Bureau of Economic Research, June 2022, https://doi.org/10.3386/w30101.

54.   Keeanga-Yamahtta Taylor, "Against Black Homeownership," *Boston Review*, November 18, 2019, https://www.bostonreview.net/articles/keeanga-yamahtta-taylor-keeanga-excerpt/.

55.   Matthew Desmond and Nathan Wilmers, "Do the Poor Pay More for Housing? Exploitation, Profit, and Risk in Rental Markets," *American Journal of Sociology* 124, no. 4 (January 2019): 1090–124, https://doi.org/10.1086/701697.

56.   Mike Davis, "The L.A. Inferno," *Socialist Review* 22, no. 1 (January 1992): 57–80. See also Mike Davis, "Who Killed Los Angeles? Part Two: The Verdict Is Given," *New Left Review*, no. 199 (June 1, 1993), 40.

57.   David Harvey, "Accumulation by Dispossession," in *The New Imperialism* (Oxford and New York: Oxford University Press, 2003), https://doi.org/10.1093/oso/9780199264315.003.0007.

58.   Javier Moreno Zacarés, "Residential Accumulation: A Political Economy Framework," *Housing, Theory and Society* 41, no. 1 (January 4, 2024): 1–23, https://doi.org/10.1080/14036096.2023.2292567.

59.   Paul Tostevin, "The Total Value of Global Real Estate," *Savills Impacts* (blog), September 9, 2021, https://www.savills.com/impacts/market-trends/the-total-value-of-global-real-estate.html.

60.   It indexes, too, the supply and demand of complex debt products and financial instruments, and of places to shield wealth from tax claims. Tom Slater, "Planetary Rent Gaps," *Antipode* 49, no. S1 (January 2017): 114–37, https://doi.org/10.1111/anti.12185.

61.   Isabella Farr, "Oceanwide's LA Tab Grows to $2.3B," Real Deal, October 29,

2021, https://therealdeal.com/la/2021/10/29/oceanwides-la-gap-swells-to-2-3b/; Kelsey Ables, "Inside the Graffiti-Covered L.A. Skyscrapers That Drew Global Attention," *Washington Post*, February 8, 2024, https://www.washingtonpost.com/entertainment/art/2024/02/08/los-angeles-graffiti-building.

62. "Homelessness: Better HUD Oversight of Data Collection Could Improve Estimates of Homeless Population," US Government Accountability Office, July 14, 2020, https://www.gao.gov/products/gao-20-433.

63. 2023 AHAR: Part 1 – PIT Estimates of Homelessness in the U.S," U.S. Department of Housing and Urban Development's Office of Policy Development and Research, December 2023, https://www.huduser.gov/portal/datasets/ahar/2023-ahar-part-1-pit-estimates-of-homelessness-in-the-us.html; Jugal K. Patel et al., "Black, Homeless and Burdened by L.A.'s Legacy of Racism," *New York Times*, December 23, 2019, https://www.nytimes.com/interactive/2019/12/22/us/los-angeles-homeless-black-residents.html.

64. "Housing Not Handcuffs: Ending the Criminalization of Homelessness in U.S. Cities," National Law Center on Homelessness and Poverty, 2019, https://homelesslaw.org/wp-content/uploads/2019/12/HOUSING-NOT-HANDCUFFS-2019-FINAL.pdf.

65. Nick Graetz et al., "The Impacts of Rent Burden and Eviction on Mortality in the United States, 2000–2019," *Social Science and Medicine* 340 (January 1, 2024): 116398, https://doi.org/10.1016/j.socscimed.2023.116398.

66. When society places its members in "such a position that they inevitably meet a too early and an unnatural death ... when it deprives thousands of the necessaries of life ... until that death ensues which is the inevitable consequence—knows that these thousands of victims must perish, and yet permits these conditions to remain, its deed is murder," Friedrich Engels once charged. See Friedrich Engels, "Results," in *The Condition of the Working Class in England*, Oxford World's Classics (Oxford and New York: Oxford University Press, 2009).

67. Cheap for us does not have to mean poorly made or maintained.

68. "The State of the Nation's Housing," Joint Center for Housing Studies of Harvard University, 2017, https://jchs.harvard.edu/sites/default/files/harvard_jchs_state_of_the_nations_housing_2017.pdf.

69. See Emily Badger, "A Luxury Apartment Rises in a Poor Neighborhood. What Happens Next?," *New York Times*, February 14, 2020, https://www.nytimes.com/2020/02/14/upshot/luxury-apartments-poor-neighborhoods.html.

70. New development may make housing more accessible, but it doesn't make it cheaper. See Eric Levitz, "Rent Growth Is Slowing (Where Housing Got Built)," *Intelligencer*, August 4, 2023, https://nymag.com/intelligencer/2023/08/rent-growth-is-slowing-where-housing-got-built.html.

71. One of the most frustrating aspects of this "debate" is that to a large extent "both sides" grant these facts. For an elegant escape valve, see Sam Stein, "The Zone Defense," *Jacobin*, June 4, 2019, https://jacobin.com/2019/06/the-zone-defense.

72. Dan Emmanuel, "The Upshot of Focusing on Extremely Low Income Renters: Expanded Housing Availability for All Renters," *On the Home Front* (blog), May 18, 2016, https://hfront.org/2016/05/18/the-upshot-of-focusing-on-extremely-low-income-renters-expanded-housing-availability-for-all-renters/.

73. Conor Dougherty and Ben Casselman, "We Need to Keep Building Houses, Even If No One Wants to Buy," *New York Times*, July 23, 2022, https://www.nytimes.com/2022/07/23/business/housing-market-crisis-supply.html.

74. Friedrich Engels, *The Housing Question* (New York: International Publishers, 2021).

75. Engels, *Housing Question*.

76. Beth Stratford, "An End to Landlordism," *Greater Manchester Housing Action* (blog), December 31, 2020, http://www.gmhousingaction.com/an-end-to-landlordism/.

77. Thank you to Michael Denning for the conversation about this and more. Also see Brooklyn Eviction Defense, which foregrounds the political subject of the "worker-tenant."

78. Chris Murphy, "Studios Allegedly Won't End Strike Till Writers 'Start Losing Their Apartments,'" *Vanity Fair*, July 12, 2023, https://www.vanityfair.com/hollywood/2023/07/studios-allegedly-wont-end-strike-til-writers-start-losing-their-apartments.

79. "In the face of stagnant growth rates, capital accumulation becomes largely zero-sum redistributive conflict in which investment flees to the safety of rentierism." Javier Moreno Zacarés, "Euphoria of the Rentier?," *New Left Review*, no. 129 (June 15, 2021): 47–67. See also David Harvey, *The Limits to Capital* (Brooklyn: Verso, 2018); Brett Christophers, *Rentier Capitalism: Who Owns the Economy, and Who Pays for It?* (London and New York: Verso, 2020); Raquel Rolnik, *Urban Warfare: Housing under the Empire*

of Finance, trans. Felipe Hirschhorn (London: Verso, 2019); and Julian Smith-Newman, "The Case for the Rent Strike," forthcoming.

80. For further analyses of the importance of the tenant movement at this juncture in history, see: David Harvey, *Rebel Cities: From the Right to the City to the Urban Revolution* (London and New York: Verso, 2019); Tara Raghuveer and John Washington, "The Case for the Tenant Union," *Poverty and Race* 32, no. 1 (March 2023), https://www.prrac.org/the-case-for-the-tenant-union-jan-mar-2023-p-r-issue/; Holden Taylor, "Who Is for Tenants?," *Brooklyn Rail*, July 12, 2022, https://brooklynrail.org/2022/07/field-notes/Who-is-for-Tenants; School of Echoes Los Angeles, "La Comuna o Nada," *Eurozine*, May 20, 2020, https://www.eurozine.com/la-comuna-o-nada/; David Stein, "'In a Good Economy Homelessness Goes Up': Inflation and the Housing Question," *LPE Project* (blog), March 21, 2022, https://lpeproject.org/blog/in-a-good-economy-homelessness-goes-up-inflation-and-the-housing-question/; Julian Francis Park, "Abolish Rent!," *Radical Housing Journal* 1, no. 2 (September 21, 2019), https://radicalhousingjournal.org/2019/abolish-rent/.

81. This sentence remixes Taylor, "Who Is for Tenants?"

Chapter 2: The War on Tenants

1. Tracy Rosenthal, "The Los Angeles City Council Scandal Is Evidence of a Long War on Tenants," *New Republic*, October 19, 2022, https://newrepublic.com/article/168195/los-angeles-city-council-scandal-evidence-long-war-tenants.

2. David Zahniser, "L.A. Has Okd $1 Billion in Tax Incentives to Developers since 2005. That Assistance Needs More Scrutiny, Controller Says," *Los Angeles Times*, August 10, 2018, https://www.latimes.com/local/lanow/la-me-ln-hotel-subsidy-report-20180810-story.html.

3. K.-Sue Park, "Conquest and Slavery in the Property Law Course: Notes for Teachers," SSRN Scholarly Paper (Rochester, NY, July 24, 2020), https://doi.org/10.2139/ssrn.3659947; Cheryl I. Harris, "Whiteness as Property," *Harvard Law Review* 106, no. 8 (June 1993): 1707, https://doi.org/10.2307/1341787.

4. For more on the relationship between settler colonialism and genocide and settler colonialism as the taking of land through the elimination of people, see Patrick Wolfe, "Settler Colonialism and the Elimination of the Native,"

Journal of Genocide Research 8, no. 4 (December 1, 2006): 387–409, https://doi.org/10.1080/14623520601056240.

5. In his history of racial terror in Kentucky, for example, historian George C. Wright notes the centrality of land dispossession. George C. Wright, *Racial Violence in Kentucky: Lynchings, Mob Rule, and "Legal Lynchings"* (Baton Rouge, LA: LSU Press, 1996), https://lsupress.org/9780807120736/racial-violence-in-kentucky/. See also "Property and Policing in Louisville, KY," Root Cause Research Center, December 2, 2023, https://storymaps.arcgis.com/stories/4add4e9971c44b7e80d20d22671b6973.

6. The fundamental racial character of homeownership policy was implied in his speech, too. Of the songs, he said, "They are the expressions of racial longing which find outlet in the living poetry and songs of our people." Herbert Hoover, "Address to the White House Conference on Home Building and Home Ownership," December 2, 1931, The American Presidency Project, https://www.presidency.ucsb.edu/documents/address-the-white-house-conference-home-building-and-home-ownership. Of course, scholars have dedicated entire books to each decade, year, and even some days of in this story, and our extremely abridged telling will be necessarily incomplete. For the twenties and thirties, see Gail Radford, *Modern Housing for America: Policy Struggles in the New Deal Era* (Chicago: University of Chicago Press, 1996); the forties and fifties: Donald Craig Parson, *Making a Better World: Public Housing, the Red Scare, and the Direction of Modern Los Angeles* (Minneapolis: University of Minnesota Press, 2005); the sixties and seventies, see Keeanga-Yamahtta Taylor, *Race for Profit: How Banks and the Real Estate Industry Undermined Black Homeownership* (Chapel Hill: University of North Carolina Press, 2019) and Kim Phillips-Fein, *Fear City: New York's Fiscal Crisis and the Rise of Austerity Politics* (New York: Metropolitan Books, 2017); the seventies and eighties: Destin Jenkins, *Bonds of Inequality: Debt and the Making of the American City* (Chicago and London: University of Chicago Press, 2021); the eighties and nineties: Neil Smith, *The New Urban Frontier: Gentrification and the Revanchist City* (London and New York: Routledge, 1996) and Edward G. Goetz, *New Deal Ruins: Race, Economic Justice, and Public Housing Policy* (Ithaca: Cornell University Press, 2013); the 2000s, see Lisa Adkins, Melinda Cooper, and Martijn Konings, *The Asset Economy* (Cambridge, UK, and Medford, MA: Polity Press, 2020).

7. John M. Gries and James S. Taylor, "How to Own Your Home: A Handbook for Prospective Home Owners (2d Edition, August 1931)," Commerce

Department, National Institute of Standards and Technology (NIST), January 1, 1931, http://dx.doi.org/10.6028/NBS.BH.17; *The FHA Story in Summary, 1934-1959* (Washington, DC: Federal Housing Administration, 1959).

8. Kirsten Moore Sheeley et al., "The Making of a Crisis: A History of Homelessness in Los Angeles," UCLA Luskin Center for History and Policy, January 2021, https://luskincenter.history.ucla.edu/wp-content/uploads/sites/66/2021/01/LCHP-The-Making-of-A-Crisis-Report.pdf.

9. Keeanga-Yamahtta Taylor, "Back Story to the Neoliberal Moment," *Souls* 14, nos. 3–4 (July 1, 2012): 185–206, https://doi.org/10.1080/10999949.2012.764836.

10. Wendy Cole, "An Apology from the National Association of REALTORS®," *Realtor Magazine*, November 19, 2020, https://www.nar.realtor/magazine/real-estate-news/commentary/an-apology-from-the-national-al-association-of-realtors.

11. Keeanga-Yamahtta Taylor, "Back Story."

12. Homer Hoyt, *One Hundred Years of Land Values in Chicago* (Creative Media Partners, LLC, 2022), ix–x, 314, 316n6; Craig Steven Wilder, *A Covenant with Color: Race and Social Power in Brooklyn*, The Columbia History of Urban Life (New York: Columbia University Press, 2000), 191.

13. In focusing solely on federal action, the story of redlining as it is often told excludes real estate as beneficiaries and designers of the policy. See Robert Gioielli, "The Tyranny of the Map: Rethinking Redlining," *The Metropole* (blog), November 3, 2022, https://themetropole.blog/2022/11/03/the-tyranny-of-the-map-rethinking-redlining/; for more on predatory inclusion and extortionary rent-to-own schemes, see Taylor, *Race for Profit*.

14. As K-Sue Park puts it, the FHA "neither unevenly distributed existing resources or new resources—some putatively neutral 'access to credit.' Rather, it created new property and new money out of the raw material of the high value that racial exclusion held for white citizens. It created mortgages *for* segregated housing." K-Sue Park, "How Did Redlining Make Money?," Just Money, September 25, 2020, https://justmoney.org/k-sue-park-how-did-redlining-make-money/.

15. Kenneth J. Sophie Jr, "Landlord-Tenant: The Medieval Concepts of Feudal Property Law Are Alive and Well in Leases of Commercial Property in Illinois, 10 J. Marshall J. of Prac. & Proc. 338 (1977)," *UIC Law Review* 10, no. 2 (Winter 1977): 338–58.

16. The members of the American Eugenics Society referred to Congress's public

housing bill as the "race suicide amendment." Laura L. Lovett, "Eugenic Housing: Redlining, Reproductive Regulation, and Suburban Development in the
United States," *WSQ: Women's Studies Quarterly* 48, no. 1 (2020): 67–83.

17.   Parson, *Making a Better World*, 65.

18.   Homer Hoyt, *According to Hoyt: Fifty Years of Homer Hoyt* (Washington,
      DC: Homer Hoyt Associates, 1966), 156.

19.   Parson, *Making a Better World*, 65.

20.   Quoted in Wilder, *A Covenant with Color*, 199.

21.   Marques A. Vestal, "Property Conflict in the Promised Land: A History of
      Black Home Struggles in Los Angeles, 1920-1950" (UCLA, 2020), https://
      escholarship.org/uc/item/9rj006gm. According to C. David Ginsburg,
      general counsel of the OPA, federal rent control saved tenants $1 billion a
      year. See Alisa Belinkoff Katz, "'People Are Simply Unable to Pay the Rent':
      What History Tells Us about Rent Control In Los Angeles," UCLA Luskin
      Center for History and Policy, October 2018, https://luskincenter.history.
      ucla.edu/wp-content/uploads/sites/66/2018/09/People-Are-Simply-Un-
      able-to-Pay-the-Rent.pdf.

22.   Lest we imagine Jewish people did not participate in leveraging race into
      real estate profit, here is the founder of Levittown, in 1947: "As a Jew, I have
      no room in my mind or heart for racial prejudice. But I have come to know
      that if we sell one house to a Negro family, then 90 or 95 percent of our white
      customers will not buy into the community. This is their attitude, not ours.
      As a company, our position is simply this: We can solve a housing problem,
      or we can try to solve a racial problem, but we cannot combine the two."
      Bruce Lambert, "At 50, Levittown Contends with Its Legacy of Bias," *New
      York Times*, December 28, 1997, https://www.nytimes.com/1997/12/28/
      nyregion/at-50-levittown-contends-with-its-legacy-of-bias.html.

23.   Parson, *Making a Better World*, 198.

24.   The reinforcing dynamic of mass consumption and homeownership was
      featured in the debate between capitalist and communist modes of produc-
      tion staged in the spectacle of the 1959 "Kitchen Debates": when then vice
      president Nixon gave Chairman Nikita Khrushchev a tour of American
      household appliances, he praised the ingenuity of planned obsolescence;
      Khrushchev dismissed the houses as built to last only twenty years. For
      more on the strategy of shirking recession by "building houses and filling
      them with things," see David Harvey, "Realization Crises and the Transfor-
      mation of Daily Life," *Space and Culture* 22, no. 2 (May 1, 2019): 126–41,

https://doi.org/10.1177/1206331218786668.

25. "A program to achieve economic and environmental justice for women requires, by definition, a solution which overcomes the traditional divisions between the house-hold and the market economy, the private dwelling and the workplace." Dolores Hayden, "What Would a Non-Sexist City Be Like? Speculations on Housing, Urban Design, and Human Work," *Signs* 5, no. 3 (1980): S170–87.

26. Quoted in Taylor, "Back Story."

27. Wilder, *A Covenant with Color*, 212.

28. The country's first zoning law, implemented in Modesto, California, in 1885, barred Chinese immigrants from areas of the city. See Marc A. Weiss, "The Rise of the Community Builders: The American Real Estate Industry and Urban Land Planning," in *Suburbia Re-examined*, ed. Barbara M. Kelly, (New York, Westport, CT, and London: Greenwood Press, 1989).

29. Sammi Aibinder and Lindsay Owens, "No Room for Rent: Addressing Rising Rent Prices through Public Investment and Public Power," Roosevelt Institute, November 2021, https://rooseveltinstitute.org/wp-content/uploads/2021/11/RI_NoRoomForRentAddressingRisingRentPrices_IssueBrief_202110.pdf.

30. F. John Devaney, "Tracking the American Dream: 50 Years of Housing History from the Census Bureau: 1940–1990," US Department of Commerce, May 1994, https://www.huduser.gov/portal/Publications/pdf/HUD-7775.pdf.

31. On the history of urban displacement, see June Manning Thomas, "Urban Displacement: Fruits of a History of Collusion," *Black Scholar* 11, no. 2 (November 1, 1979): 68–77, https://doi.org/10.1080/00064246.1979.11414074.

32. Chavez Ravine itself was a product of forced (and subsidized) relocation, as 250 Mexican American families fled LA River floods. See "Settlement Losing Battle for Its Life. Bitter Residents of Chavez Ravine Slowly Yield to Housing Project," *Los Angeles Times*, August 20, 1951, https://www.news-papers.com/article/the-los-angeles-times/28301162/.

33. John H. M. Laslett, *Shameful Victory: The Los Angeles Dodgers, the Red Scare, and the Hidden History of Chavez Ravine* (Tucson: University of Arizona Press, 2015), 3, 39, 66–69.

34. Thomas S. Hines, "Housing, Baseball, and Creeping Socialism: The Battle of Chavez Ravine, Los Angeles, 1949–1959," *Journal*

of Urban History 8, no. 2 (February 1, 1982): 123–43, https://doi.
org/10.1177/009614428200800201; Nathan Masters, "Chavez Ravine:
Community to Controversial Real Estate," *PBS SoCal*, September 13,
2012, https://www.pbssocal.org/shows/lost-la/chavez-ravine-communi-
ty-to-controversial-real-estate.

35. Brent Cebul, "Tearing Down Black America," *Boston Review*, July 22, 2020,
https://www.bostonreview.net/articles/brent-cebul-tearing-down-black-
america/.

36. Donald Craig Parson, *Making a Better World: Public Housing, the Red Scare,
and the Direction of Modern Los Angeles* (Minneapolis: University of Minnesota Press, 2005), 199.

37. "If race has no essence," Ruth Wilson Gilmore writes, "racism does." Ruth
Wilson Gilmore, "Fatal Couplings of Power and Difference: Notes on
Racism and Geography," in *Abolition Geography: Essays towards Liberation*,
ed. Brenna Bhandar and Alberto Toscano, (London and New York: Verso,
2022), 136; see also Prentiss A. Dantzler, "The Urban Process under Racial
Capitalism: Race, Anti-Blackness, and Capital Accumulation," *Journal of
Race, Ethnicity and the City* 2, no. 2 (July 3, 2021): 113–34, https://doi.org/
10.1080/26884674.2021.1934201.

38. Elizabeth Kai Hinton, *America on Fire: The Untold History of Police Violence
and Black Rebellion since the 1960s*, 1st ed. (New York: Liveright Publishing, a division of W. W. Norton, 2021).

39. Quoted in Jelani Cobb, "A Warning Ignored," *New York Review of Books*,
August 19, 2021, https://www.nybooks.com/articles/2021/08/19/kern-
er-commission-warning-ignored/.

40. James Boggs and Stephen M. Ward, *Pages from a Black Radical's Notebook:
A James Boggs Reader*, African American Life Series (Detroit: Wayne State
University Press, 2011), 302. Also see "The City Is a Black Man's Land" in
that volume.

41. Racial bias in housing has been notoriously difficult to prosecute. In 1968,
the Contract Buyers' League sued fifty real estate brokers and banks for
violations of fair housing. Dismissing the case, the presiding judge asserted,
"Council for plaintiffs have not painted a pretty picture of the defendants,
but the picture is one of exploitation for profit, not racial discrimination."
Quoted in Keeanga-Yamahtta Taylor, "Back Story."

42. A. K. Sandoval-Strausz, "Latino Landscapes: Postwar Cities and the Trans-
national Origins of a New Urban America," *Journal of American History* 101,

no. 3 (December 1, 2014): 804–31, https://doi.org/10.1093/jahist/jau657.

43. Johanna Fernández, *The Young Lords: A Radical History* (Chapel Hill: University of North Carolina Press, 2020).

44. Mike Davis, *Magical Urbanism: Latinos Reinvent the US City*, rev. and expanded ed., The Haymarket Series (London: Verso, 2007).

45. Ronald Lawson, ed., *The Tenant Movement in New York City, 1904–1984* (New Brunswick, NJ: Rutgers University Press, 1986).

46. "Our urban system is based on the theory of taking the peasant and turning him into an industrial worker. Now there are no industrial jobs. Why not keep him a peasant?" asked New York's Housing and Development Administration chief. Kevin Baker, "The Death of a Once Great City," *Harper's*, July 2018, https://harpers.org/archive/2018/07/the-death-of-new-york-city-gentrification/.

47. "'Devolution'—the name for structural adjustment in richer, inequality-riven polities." Ruth Wilson Gilmore and Craig Gilmore, "Beyond Bratton," in *Abolition Geography*, 304. See also: Agis Salpukas, "Moratorium on Housing Subsidy Spells Hardship for Thousands," *New York Times*, April 16, 1973, sec. archives, https://www.nytimes.com/1973/04/16/archives/moratorium-on-housing-subsidy-spells-hardship-for-thousands-stricter.html.

48. See "Homegrown Revolution" in Mike Davis, *City of Quartz: Excavating the Future in Los Angeles* (London: Verso, 1991).

49. At the time, the homeowners' lobby went by the Apartment Association of Los Angeles County; this name is still sometimes in use. For a laugh, see "History," AAGLA, February 1, 2017, https://aagla.org/history/.

50. Prop 13's present benefits continue to accrue most in wealthy neighborhoods. After its passage, California dropped from fifth in per-student funding for public schools to forty-seventh in the nation. Prop 13 has also been credited with the rise of urban entrepreneurialism as well as its prison boom. See "Common Claims about Proposition 13," Legislative Analyst's Office, September 19, 2016, https://lao.ca.gov/publications/report/3497; Jacob Denney, Phil Levin, and Susannah Parsons, "Burdens and Benefits: Investigating Prop. 13's Unequal Impacts in Oakland," The Tax Fairness Project, November 2021, https://www.spur.org/sites/default/files/2022-02/SPUR_Burdens_and_Benefits.pdf; Carrie Hahnel et al., "How Proposition 13 Has Contributed to Intergenerational, Economic, and Racial Inequities in Schools and Communities," Opportunity Institute, June 2022, https://static1.squarespace.com/static/55f70367e4b0974cf2b82009/t/62b34bd-

319072b7c70d02020/1655917530375/OI%2Breport%2Bprop%2B13%2B-
final.pdf; John J. Kirlin and Anne M. Kirlin, "Public Choices – Private
Resources: Financing Capital Infrastructure for California's Growth
through Public-Private Bargaining," California Tax Foundation, July 1982,
https://www.caltax.org/foundation/reports/1982-Public-Choices-Pri-
vate-Resources.pdf; and Ruth Wilson Gilmore, *Golden Gulag: Prisons, Sur-
plus, Crisis, and Opposition in Globalizing California*, (Berkeley: University of
California Press, 2007).

51.   Destin Jenkins, *The Bonds of Inequality: Debt and the Making of the American City* (Chicago and London: University of Chicago Press, 2021).

52.   Kim Phillips-Fein, *Fear City*.

53.   Tracy Rosenthal, "The Enduring Fiction of Affordable Housing," *New
Republic*, April 2, 2021, https://newrepublic.com/article/161806/afford-
able-housing-public-housing-rent-los-angeles.

54.   Mike Davis, "Who Killed LA? A Political Autopsy," *New Left Review*, no. 197
(January 1993): 11; Peter Dreier, "Reagan's Real Legacy," *The Nation*, February 4, 2011, https://www.thenation.com/article/archive/reagans-real-legacy/.

55.   Beth Rubin, James Wright, and Joel Devine, "Unhousing the Urban
Poor: The Reagan Legacy," *Journal of Sociology and Social Welfare* 19, no.
1 (March 1, 1992), https://doi.org/10.15453/0191-5096.2013; Edward
G. Goetz, "Potential Effects of Federal Policy Devolution on Local Housing Expenditures," *CrossRef Listing of Deleted DOIs* 25, no. 3 (1995): 99,
https://doi.org/10.2307/3330689.

56.   Jonathan Kozol, *Rachel and Her Children: Homeless Families in America*
(New York: Crown Publishers, 1988), 14–15.

57.   Mimi Kirk, "What Causes Homelessness? Start with Capitalism.,"
Bloomberg, May 13, 2020, https://www.bloomberg.com/news/arti-
cles/2020-05-13/what-causes-homelessness-start-with-capitalism.

58.   Stephanie Chavez and James Quinn, "Substandard Housing : Garages:
Immigrants In, Cars Out," *Los Angeles Times*, May 24, 1987, https://www.
latimes.com/archives/la-xpm-1987-05-24-mn-2558-story.html.

59.   Ruth Wilson Gilmore, *Golden Gulag*.

60.   See Anne Bonds, "Race and Ethnicity I: Property, Race, and the Carceral
State," *Progress in Human Geography* 43, no. 3 (June 1, 2019): 574–83,
https://doi.org/10.1177/0309132517751297.

61.   Race and class "proved a more powerful predictor of perceived disorder than
did carefully observed disorder." Stephen W. Raudenbush and Robert J. Samp-

son, "Seeing Disorder: Neighborhood Stigma and the Social Construction of 'Broken Windows,'" *Social Psychology Quarterly* 67, no. 4 (2004): 319–36.

62. George L. Kelling and James Q. Wilson, "Broken Windows," *Atlantic*, March 1, 1982, https://www.theatlantic.com/magazine/archive/1982/03/broken-windows/304465/.

63. William Bratton's first broken windows policy, implemented under Rudy Guliani, was known as "Police Strategy No. 5: Reclaiming the Public Spaces." As Bratton put it in 2003, "The homeless take over a portion of the park. Drug dealers follow. Drug dealers beget violence. It then begins to affect the whole business area and businesses begin to die." Richard Winton and Kristina Sauerwein, "LAPD Tests New Policing Strategy," *Los Angeles Times*, February 2, 2003, https://www.latimes.com/archives/la-xpm-2003-feb-02-me-revive2-story.html.

64. Margaret M. Ramírez, "City as Borderland: Gentrification and the Policing of Black and Latinx Geographies in Oakland," *Environment and Planning D: Society and Space* 38, no. 1 (February 1, 2020): 147–66, https://doi.org/10.1177/0263775819843924; Adolfo Flores, "A Court Made It Illegal for This Guy to Be Seen with His Dad in Public and Now He's Fighting Back," *BuzzFeed News*, March 14, 2017, https://www.buzzfeednews.com/article/adolfoflores/life-under-a-gang-injunction; ACLU of Southern California, "Court Issues Historic Ruling against Gang Injunctions in L.A.," March 15, 2018, https://www.aclusocal.org/en/press-releases/court-issues-historic-ruling-against-gang-injunctions-la.

65. Kim Phillips-Fein, "'My High-Income Earners,'" *New York Review of Books* (blog), December 20, 2022, https://www.nybooks.com/online/2022/12/20/my-high-income-earners-new-york/.

66. Sammi Aibinder and Lindsay Owens, "No Room for Rent: Addressing Rising Rent Prices through Public Investment and Public Power," Roosevelt Institute, November 2021, https://rooseveltinstitute.org/wp-content/uploads/2021/11/RI_NoRoomForRentAddressingRisingRentPrices_IssueBrief_202110.pdf.

67. Goetz, *New Deal Ruins*. For an excellent history of the destruction of public housing in LA, see Jacob Woocher, "LA's War on Public Housing: An Introduction," *Knock LA*, September 4, 2023, https://knock-la.com/los-angeles-war-on-public-housing-introduction/.

68. Prasanna Rajasekaran, Mark Treskon, and Solomon Greene, *What Does the Research Tell Us about the Effectiveness of Local Action?* Urban Institute, Jan-

uary 2019, https://www.urban.org/sites/default/files/publication/99646/rent_control._what_does_the_research_tell_us_about_the_effectiveness_of_local_action_1.pdf.

69. "The Morning After," *Economist*, April 30, 1998, https://www.economist.com/united-states/1998/04/30/the-morning-after.

70. REITs pool investments and can be bought and sold like stocks; asset managers pool investments for a fixed or flexible term. Both can be publicly traded or privately sought. See Brett Christophers, *Our Lives in Their Portfolios: Why Asset Managers Own the World* (London and New York: Verso, 2023).

71. Herman Schwartz, "Finance and the State in the Housing Bubble," in *Subprime Cities*, ed. Manuel B. Aalbers, 1st ed. (Wiley, 2012), 53–73, https://doi.org/10.1002/9781444347456.ch2.

72. Francesca Mari, "A $60 Billion Housing Grab by Wall Street," *New York Times*, March 4, 2020, https://www.nytimes.com/2020/03/04/magazine/wall-street-landlords.html.

73. Peter Whoriskey, Spencer Woodman, and Margot Gibbs, "This Block Used to Be for First-Time Homebuyers. Then Global Investors Bought In," *Washington Post*, December 15, 2021, https://www.washingtonpost.com/business/interactive/2021/investors-rental-foreclosure/.

74. As Adkins et al. argue, "Middle class politics of asset democratization has ended up undermining the conditions of its own viability." Adkins et al., *The Asset Economy*, 90; Patrick Clark, "Renters Now Rule Half of U.S. Cities," *Bloomberg*, March 23, 2017, https://www.bloomberg.com/news/articles/2017-03-23/renters-now-rule-half-of-u-s-cities.

75. Synthesized from "The Developer President and the Private Side of Planning History" in Stein, *Capital City*, 135–78. See also Michael Denning on Trump's populism and the real estate crisis: "If Bonaparte and Trump are 'populists,' it is less because they appealed to the people than because they rose to power in the struggle over social forms of exploitation: debt, rent and mortgage." Michael Denning, "Impeachment as a Social Form," *New Left Review*, no. 122 (April 17, 2020): 65–79.

76. Samuel Stein, *Capital City: Gentrification and the Real Estate State*, Jacobin Series (London and Brooklyn, NY: Verso, 2019).

77. See David Stein, "'In a Good Economy Homelessness Goes Up': Inflation and the Housing Question," *LPE Project* (blog), March 21, 2022, https://lpeproject.org/blog/in-a-good-economy-homelessness-goes-up-inflation-and-the-housing-question/.

78. Neil Smith, "Toward a Theory of Gentrification: A Back to the City
     Movement by Capital, Not People," *Journal of the American Plan-
     ning Association* 45, no. 4 (October 1979): 538–48, https://doi.
     org/10.1080/01944367908977002.

79. Jesse Drucker and Eric Lipton, "How a Trump Tax Break to Help Poor
     Communities Became a Windfall for the Rich," *New York Times*, August
     31, 2019, https://www.nytimes.com/2019/08/31/business/tax-opportuni-
     ty-zones.html.

80. Elizabeth Kneebone, "The Changing Geography of US Poverty: Testimony
     before the House Ways and Means Committee, Subcommittee on Human
     Resources," Brookings, February 15, 2017, https://www.brookings.edu/
     articles/the-changing-geography-of-us-poverty/.

81. For a comprehensive account of the role of policing in LA land grabs, see
     Automating Banishment: The Surveillance and Policing of Looted Land, Stop
     LAPD Spying, November 2021, https://automatingbanishment.org/
     assets/AUTOMATING-BANISHMENT.pdf.

82. Don Mitchell, *Mean Streets: Homelessness, Public Space, and the Limits
     of Capital* (Athens, GA: University of Georgia Press, 2020), https://doi.
     org/10.2307/j.ctvqmp379, 98; Sara Shortt, "Op-Ed: We Don't Need Pro-
     tection from the Homeless. They Need Protection from Us," *Los Angeles
     Times*, October 15, 2018, https://www.latimes.com/opinion/op-ed/la-oe-
     shortt-homeless-victims-20181015-story.html.

83. "Housing Not Handcuffs: Ending the Criminalization of Homelessness
     in U.S. Cities," National Law Center on Homelessness and Poverty, 2019,
     https://homelesslaw.org/wp-content/uploads/2019/12/HOUSING-
     NOT-HANDCUFFS-2019-FINAL.pdf.

84. Liam Dillon, Ben Poston, and Julia Barajas, "Black and Latino Renters Face
     Eviction, Exclusion amid Police Crackdowns in California," *Los Angeles
     Times*, November 19, 2020, https://www.latimes.com/homeless-housing/
     story/2020-11-19/california-housing-policies-hurt-black-latino-renters;
     Samantha Michaels, "Hundreds of Cities Have Adopted a New Strategy
     for Reducing Crime in Housing. Is It Making Neighborhoods Safer—or
     Whiter?" *Mother Jones*, December 2019, https://www.motherjones.com/
     criminal-justice/2019/10/crime-free-housing-making-neighborhoods-saf-
     er-or-whiter/.

85. In the Valley's self-described "war on Section 8," tenants' family and
     romantic partners, social gatherings, even clothing choices became

grounds for Black tenants to be stripped of vouchers and displaced. Rahim
Kurwa, "The New *Man in the House* Rules: How the Regulation of Housing
Vouchers Turns Personal Bonds into Eviction Liabilities," *Housing Policy
Debate* 30, no. 6 (November 1, 2020): 926–49, https://doi.org/10.1080/1
0511482.2020.1778056. Also thank you to Rahim Kurwa for early access
to his yet-untitled book manuscript. Abby Sewell, "L.A. County to Pay $2
Million to Antelope Valley Housing Discrimination Victims," *Los Angeles
Times*, July 20, 2015, https://www.latimes.com/local/lanow/la-me-ln-an-
telope-valley-settlement-20150720-story.html.

86. Terra Graziani et al., "Property, Personhood, and Police: The Making of
     Race and Space through Nuisance Law," *Antipode* 54 (October 27, 2021),
     https://doi.org/10.1111/anti.12792.

87. This section condenses evidence from the masterful study by the
     Root Cause Research Center: "Property and Policing in Louisville,
     KY" (December 2, 2023), https://storymaps.arcgis.com/stories/4ad-
     d4e9971c44b7e80d20d22671b6973.

88. Matthew Desmond, *Poverty, by America*, 1st ed. (New York: Crown, 2023),
     91; Peter Wagner and Bernadette Rabuy, "Following the Money of Mass
     Incarceration," Prison Policy Initiative, January 25, 2017, https://www.
     prisonpolicy.org/reports/money.html.

89. Desmond, *Poverty, by America*, 91.

90. Evan Calder Williams, "In Love and Memory," *New Inquiry*, April 22, 2015,
     https://thenewinquiry.com/blog/in-love-and-memory/.

Chapter 3: The Return of the Rent Strike

1.   Louis Sahagún, "Boyle Heights: Problems, Pride and Promise," *Los Angeles
     Times*, July 31, 1983, https://www.latimes.com/california/story/2020-08-
     26/boyle-heights-problems-pride-and-promise.

2.   This struggle is the origin of Union de Vecinos, and thus in many ways, LATU.
     See Jacob Woocher, "Pico-Aliso: We Shall Not Be Moved," *Knock LA*, Septem-
     ber 5, 2023, https://knock-la.com/pico-aliso-we-shall-not-be-moved/.

3.   Kean O'Brien, Leonardo Vilchis, and Corina Maritescu, "Boyle Heights
     and the Fight against Gentrification as State Violence," *American Quarterly*
     71, no. 2 (2019): 389–96.

4.   Gilbert Estrada, "The Historical Roots of Gentrification in Boyle Heights,"
     PBS SoCal, September 13, 2017, https://www.pbssocal.org/shows/city-ris-

ing/the-historical-roots-of-gentrification-in-boyle-heights.

5.   Union de Vecinos officially merged with the LA Tenants Union in 2019,
     becoming its Eastside local chapter. Because their organizers, meeting
     space, and infrastructure overlapped from the start, we refer to them as the
     same entity throughout this chapter.

6.   For more on the false promises of "affordable housing," see chapter four.

7.   Isa Ramirez, interview by Tracy Rosenthal and Leonardo Vilchis, Los
     Angeles, August 2022.

8.   Melissa Reyes, interview by Tracy Rosenthal and Leonardo Vilchis, Los
     Angeles, August 2022.

9.   "Interview: BJ Turner, Founder of Real Estate Investment and Devel-
     opment Firm Dunleer," *Dunleer Group* (blog), July 6, 2021, https://
     dunleergroup.com/post/interview-bj-turner-founder-of-real-estate-invest-
     ment-and-development-firm-dunleer/.

10. Jason McGahan, "Mariachis Are Getting Priced Out of Boyle Heights," *LA
     Weekly*, April 26, 2017, https://www.laweekly.com/mariachis-are-getting-
     priced-out-of-boyle-heights/.

11. Ramirez, interview.

12. Reema Khrais, "The Mariachi Rent Strike," December 16, 2021, in *This
     Is Uncomfortable*, produced by Hayley Hershman et al., 32:25, pod-
     cast, https://www.marketplace.org/shows/this-is-uncomfortable-ree-
     ma-khrais/the-mariachi-rent-strike/.

13. Jacob Woocher, "Union de Vecinos: 25 Years of Impact on LA's Tenants
     Movement," Knock LS, August 23, 2021, https://knock-la.com/union-de-
     vecinos-25-years-los-angeles-tenants-movement/.

14. Khrais, "Mariachi Rent Strike."

15. Frances Fox Piven and Richard Cloward, *Poor People's Movements: Why
     They Succeed, How They Fail* (New York: Knopf Doubleday Publishing
     Group, 1979), 24.

16. Robert M. Fogelson, *The Great Rent Wars: New York, 1917–1929* (New
     Haven: Yale University Press, 2014); Rane Stark-Buhl, "Here Is a Rent
     Strike: 1919 Red Scare and the NYC Tenant Movement, 1918-1920," May
     11, 2023, https://storymaps.arcgis.com/stories/d85745143f81470d94f-
     741677c3d71d4.

17. Philip Mattera and Donna Demac, *Developing and Underdeveloping New
     York: The "Fiscal Crisis" and a Strategy for Fighting Austerity* (Brooklyn,
     NY: New York Struggle Against Work, 1976), http://zerowork.org/

NYSAWDemacMatteraNYC.pdf.

18. Jason McGahan, "Boyle Heights Mariachis Take a Win against an 80% Rent Hike," *L.A. Taco*, February 16, 2018, https://lataco.com/boyle-heights-mariachis-take-win-80-rent-hike.

19. Ramirez, interview.

20. Ramirez, interview.

21. Molly Lambert, "The Rent Strike That Sparked a Movement," *The Land*, February 5, 2019, https://thelandmag.com/mariachi-plaza-rent-strike-defend-boyle-heights/.

22. Jason McGahan, "Facing Eviction, Boyle Heights Mariachis Are Going to Court," *LA Weekly*, September 13, 2017, https://www.laweekly.com/facing-eviction-boyle-heights-mariachis-are-going-to-court/.

23. Elizabeth Blaney, interview with Tracy Rosenthal and Leonardo Vilchis, Los Angeles, August 2022.

24. Blaney, interview.

25. Blaney, interview.

26. Ruben Vives, "As Rents Soar in L.A., Even Boyle Heights' Mariachis Sing the Blues," *Los Angeles Times*, September 9, 2017, https://www.latimes.com/local/lanow/la-me-boyle-heights-musicians-gentrification-20170909-htmlstory.html.

27. Khrais, "The Mariachi Rent Strike."

28. Blaney, interview.

29. McGahan, "Boyle Heights Mariachis."

30. Blaney, interview.

31. Khrais, "Mariachi Rent Strike."

32. Reyes, interview.

Chapter 4: La Lucha Educa

1. Conor Dougherty, "Who Will Stand Up for Renters? Their Elected Representatives, Who Also Rent," *New York Times*, July 21, 2023, https://www.nytimes.com/2023/07/21/business/economy/renters-caucus-elected-representatives-who-rent.html.

2. Robert M. Fogelson, *The Great Rent Wars: New York, 1917–1929* (New Haven: Yale University Press, 2014).

3. Philip Mattera and Donna Demac, *Developing and Underdeveloping New York: The "Fiscal Crisis" and a Strategy for Fighting Austerity* (Brooklyn,

NY: New York Struggle Against Work, 1976), http://zerowork.org/NYSAWDemacMatteraNYC.pdf.

4. Elizabeth Popp Berman, *Thinking like an Economist: How Efficiency Replaced Equality in U.S. Public Policy* (Princeton: Princeton University Press, 2023).

5. Ruth Wilson Gilmore, "In the Shadow of the Shadow State," in *Abolition Geography: Essays towards Liberation*, ed. Brenna Bhandar and Alberto Toscano (London and New York: Verso, 2022).

6. Jane McAlevey, *No Shortcuts: Organizing for Power in the New Gilded Age* (New York: Oxford University Press, 2016).

7. For a review of these constraints in recent tenant organizing in NYC, see Holden Taylor, "Who Is for Tenants?," *The Brooklyn Rail*, July 12, 2022, https://brooklynrail.org/2022/07/field-notes/Who-is-for-Tenants; Justin Gilmore, "Class Organization and Rupture on the Terrain of Housing," *Spectre Journal*, May 26, 2020, https://spectrejournal.com/class-organization-and-rupture-on-the-terrain-of-housing/.

8. Inés Alcazar, interview by Leonardo Vilchis, Los Angeles, September 2022.

9. James Queally, "L.A. City Councilman Curren Price Challenges Perjury, Embezzlement Charges," *Los Angeles Times*, October 13, 2023, https://www.latimes.com/california/story/2023-10-13/la-city-councilman-curren-price-challenges-perjury-embezzlement-charges.

10. James Queally, Julia Wick, and Dakota Smith, "L.A. City Councilmember Curren Price Charged with Embezzlement and Perjury," *Los Angeles Times*, June 13, 2023, https://www.latimes.com/california/story/2023-06-13/l-a-city-councilmember-curren-price-charged-with-embezzlement-perjury.

11. Alcazar, interview.

12. Alcazar, interview.

13. Alcazar, interview.

14. Alcazar, interview.

15. Mindy Thompson Fullilove, *Root Shock: How Tearing up City Neighborhoods Hurts America, and What We Can Do about It* (New York: New Village Press, 2016).

16. Tony Ramirez, interview by Leonardo Vilchis, Los Angeles, September 2022.

17. Ramirez, interview.

18. Ramirez, interview.

19. "Jobs are harder and costlier to create than voting rolls. The eradication of slums housing millions is complex far beyond integrating buses and lunch

counters." Martin Luther King, Coretta Scott King, and Vincent Harding, *Where Do We Go from Here: Chaos or Community?*, The King Legacy Series (Boston: Beacon Press, 2010), 5–6.

20. Martin Luther King et al., *Where Do We Go from Here*, 139.

21. Maria Gomez, interview by Leonardo Vilchis, Los Angeles, September 2022.

22. Left in the Bay, "Who Owns the Park?" *Verso* (blog), August 11, 2022, https://www.versobooks.com/blogs/news/5398-who-owns-the-park.

23. "Trees Planted in Poor Neighborhood Mature Just in Time for Gentrification," *The Onion*, September 10, 2015, https://www.theonion.com/trees-planted-in-poor-neighborhood-mature-just-in-time-1819592337.

24. See Janis Yue and Promise Li, "Abolition and Tenant Power in Chinatown," *Spectre Journal*, September 18, 2023, https://spectrejournal.com/aboli-tion-and-tenant-power-in-chinatown/.

25. Jack Ross, "In Los Angeles, a Friendship Grows Out of Housing Strife," *Capital and Main*, March 21, 2023, https://capitalandmain.com/in-los-an-geles-a-friendship-grows-out-of-housing-strife.

26. "23. Neil Kadisha," *Los Angeles Business Journal*, September 9, 2022, https://labusinessjournal.com/special-editions/wealthiest-angelenos/wealthiest-2022/23-neil-kadisha/.

27. Sam Trinh, interview by Tracy Rosenthal and Leonardo Vilchis, Los Ange-les, June 2022.

28. Jack Ross and Bobbi Murray, "While an Industry Feeds on the Destruction of Rent Control, Help Is on the Way," *Capital and Main*, April 11, 2022, https://capitalandmain.com/while-an-industry-feeds-on-the-destruction-of-rent-control-help-is-on-the-way.

29. Trinh, interview.

30. Trinh, interview.

31. Trinh, interview.

32. "Resisting Social Cleansing in Los Angeles: The Origins of the K3 Tenant Council (Alpine LA Properties)," Alpine LA Properties • K3 Tenant Coun-cil, https://www.k3tc.org/origins-origenes.

33. Trinh, interview.

34. Paulo Freire, *Pedagogy of the Oppressed*, 30th anniversary ed. (New York: Continuum, 2000).

35. Freire, *Pedagogy of the Oppressed*, 65. See also Mike Parker and Martha Gru-elle's critique of "a cannon-fodder version of organizing" in Mike Parker and Martha Gruelle, *Democracy Is Power* (Chicago: Labor Notes, 1999).

36. Charles M. Payne, *I've Got the Light of Freedom: The Organizing Tradition and the Mississippi Freedom Struggle* (Berkeley: University of California Press, 2007).

37. Myles Horton and Paulo Freire, *We Make the Road by Walking: Conversations on Education and Social Change* (Philadelphia: Temple University Press, 1990).

38. *Block by Block: To a World without Rent*, vol. 6, Naming the Moment (Los Angeles Tenants Union, 2022), https://latenantsunion.org/en/2023/01/23/naming-the-moment-2022/.

39. LATU Tenant Inquiry Committee, interview by Tracy Rosenthal, August 2023.

40. Mike Davis, "Old Gods, New Enigmas," *Catalyst Journal* 1, no. 2 (Summer 2017), https://catalyst-journal.com/2017/11/historical-agency-davis.

41. John L. Hammond, "Mística, Meaning and Popular Education in the Brazilian Landless Workers Movement," *Interface* 6, no. 1 (May 2014): 372–91.

42. "In revolutionary activity the changing of oneself coincides with the changing of circumstances." Karl Marx and Friedrich Engels, *The German Ideology: Including "Theses on Feuerbach" and "Introduction to the Critique of Political Economy"* (Amherst, NY: Prometheus Books, 2008), 230.

43. Freire, *Pedagogy of the Oppressed*, 92.

44. Alcazar, interview.

Chapter 5: From Housing Struggle to Land Struggle

1.   Yesenia, interview by Tracy Rosenthal and Leonardo Vilchis, Los Angeles, June 2022.

2.   Isabel Garcia, interview by Tracy Rosenthal and Leonardo Vilchis, Los Angeles, June 2022.

3.   "Where we fight is where the state is," as Ruth Wilson Gilmore and Craig Gilmore put it. Ruth Wilson Gilmore and Craig Gilmore, "Restating the Obvious," in *Abolition Geography: Essays towards Liberation* (London and New York: Verso, 2022).

4.   Tracy Rosenthal, "The Enduring Fiction of Affordable Housing," *The New Republic*, April 2, 2021, https://newrepublic.com/article/161806/affordable-housing-public-housing-rent-los-angeles.

5.   Rosenthal, "The Enduring Fiction."

6.   "Policy Basics: Project-Based Vouchers," Center on Budget and Policy Priorities, July 11, 2023, https://www.cbpp.org/research/housing/pol-

icy-basics-project-based-vouchers; Matthew Haag, "25 Million Applications: The Scramble for N.Y.C. Affordable Housing," *New York Times,* June 15, 2020, https://www.nytimes.com/2020/06/15/nyregion/nyc-affordable-housing-lottery.html.

7. Office of Policy Development and Research, "Understanding Whom the LIHTC Serves: Data on Tenants in LIHTC Units as of December 31, 2017," US Department of Housing and Urban Development, December 2019, https://www.huduser.gov/portal/sites/default/files/pdf/LIHTC-TenantReport-2017.pdf.

8. "Inside the Fight at Hillside Villa: Multiracial, Multigenerational Tenants in Chinatown Organize for Housing Justice," Hillside Villa Tenants Association, https://hillsidevillata.org/organizing-history.

9. Leslie Hernandez, interview by Tracy Rosenthal, Los Angeles, March 2021.

10. Los Angeles Tenants Union, "Here with Hillside Villa . . . ," Facebook, September 15, 2019, https://www.facebook.com/latenantsunion/videos/363239007916153/.

11. MATHEWS v. ARROW WOOD LLC, No. EDCV-07-1316-SGL (United States District Court, C.D. California April 2, 2009).

12. Hernandez, interview.

13. "2022 Major Projects/NPP/EQ, HHH Income Schedule," Los Angeles Housing and Community Investment Department, August 1, 2022, https://lahousing.lacity.org/AAHR/Documents/AMI%20Income%20and%20Rent%20Limits.pdf.

14. Laureen D. Hom, "Symbols of Gentrification? Narrating Displacement in Los Angeles Chinatown," *Urban Affairs Review* 58, no. 1 (2020): 196–228, https://doi.org/10.1177/1078087420954917.

15. Hillside Villa Tenants Association to Thomas, Chloe, and Nolan Botz, "We, the Tenants at 636 N. Hill Place, Los Angeles, CA 90012 . . . ," February 5, 2019, https://drive.google.com/file/d/1cvjhGKKBv_kKt-1BLkS58ST13xjjvYD3e/view.

16. Joe Rihn, "Can Eminent Domain Preserve L.A.'s Affordable Housing?," *Capital and Main*, February 21, 2020, https://capitalandmain.com/can-eminent-domain-preserve-los-angeles-affordable-housing-0221.

17. "Housing Advocates File Lawsuit against Property Owner Threatening Eviction by July 31," Legal Aid Foundation of Los Angeles, June 18, 2019, https://lafla.org/press-release/housing-advocates-file-lawsuit-against-property-owner-threatening-eviction/.

18. Hillside Villa Tenants Association to Councilmember Cedillo, "RE: Keeping the Hillside Villa Apartments Permanently Affordable," May 3, 2019, https://drive.google.com/file/d/1R3a7cN1RllWLctKqMmISvX-Qtsxhn5XWU/view.

19. Adela Cortez, interview by Tracy Rosenthal, Los Angeles, March 2021.

20. Hernandez, interview.

21. Ben Tansey, "Covenant Dispute in Chinatown Prompts New Legislation," *South Pasadenan*, January 31, 2020, https://southpasadenan.com/covenant-dispute-in-chinatown-prompts-new-legislation/.

22. Gina Silva, "Chinatown Landlord Gearing for Ugly Battle with City over Rising Rents," *Fox 11 Los Angeles*, February 5, 2020, https://www.foxla.com/news/chinatown-landlord-gearing-for-ugly-battle-with-city-over-rising-rents.

23. Hernandez, interview.

24. Gilbert A. Cedillo, "Hillside Villa Motion," Office of the City Clerk, January 31, 2020, https://clkrep.lacity.org/onlinedocs/2020/20-0148_mot_01-31-2020.pdf.

25. Gustavo Arellano, "Column: On LAPD Spending, Everyone's Right and Everyone's Wrong," *Los Angeles Times*, February 18, 2023, https://www.latimes.com/california/story/2023-02-18/lapd-spending-los-angeles-budget; Stop LAPD Spying and Free Radicals, *LAPD's Budget Creep* (Los Angeles: Stop LAPD Spying, 2021), https://stoplapdspying.org/zine-lapds-budget-creep/.

26. Steve Lopez, "Column: Evictions Loom for Chinatown Residents Who Can't Find Affordable Housing," *Los Angeles Times*, June 22, 2019, https://www.latimes.com/local/california/la-me-lopez-chinatown-apartment-evictions-20190622-story.html.

27. Michael H. Leifer to President Martinez and the Los Angeles City Council, "Re: Hillside Villa Apartments (Council File No. 21-0600-S101); Inaccurate Statement and Misinformation in May 9, 2022 LAHD Report Regarding Section 8 Tenants, and Wasteful Recommendation Based on Such Error," May 23, 2022, https://clkrep.lacity.org/onlinedocs/2021/21-0600-S101_misc_BFC_052422.pdf.

28. Honorable Eric Garcetti to Heleen Ramirez, Legislative Coordinator, "Council Transmittal: Report Back from the Los Angeles Housing + Community Investment Department," June 12, 2020, https://clkrep.lacity.org/onlinedocs/2020/20-0148_rpt_mayor_06-24-2020.pdf.

29. Hillside Villa Tenants Association, "New Retaliation from Botz . . . ," X

(formerly Twitter), July 8, 2022, https://twitter.com/hillside_villa/sta-
tus/1545604442321350661?s=20&t=YswXXw4z9UO4YVVl7OxliA.

30. Hillside Villa Tenants Association, "New Retaliation from Botz...," X
     (formerly Twitter), July 8, 2022, https://twitter.com/hillside_villa/sta-
     tus/1545604442321350661?s=20&t=YswXXw4z9UO4YVVl7OxliA.

31. Hillside Villa Tenants Association, "URGENT CALL TO ACTION! Take
     One Minute to Call Flores Artscape Today!," Instagram, July 13, 2022,
     https://www.instagram.com/p/Cf9RtIYvB5E/?img_index=1.

32. Joe Rihn, "Can Eminent Domain Preserve L.A.'s Affordable Housing?"
     Capital and Main, February 21, 2020, https://capitalandmain.com/
     can-eminent-domain-preserve-los-angeles-affordable-housing-0221.

33. Danielle M. Mazzella, "Affordable Homes at Risk," California Housing
     Partnership, February 2022, https://chpc.net/resources/affordable-homes-
     at-risk-2022-report/.

34. David Wagner and Phoenix Tso, "LA Approves 'Unprecedented' Plan To
     Take Over Chinatown Apartment Building, Against Owner's Wishes,"
     LAist, May 27, 2022, https://laist.com/news/housing-homelessness/
     hillside-villa-chinatown-apartment-affordable-housing-eminent-do-
     main-city-council-los-angeles-tom-botz-tenants-landlord.

35. Jack Ross, "Hillside Villa Tenants Face Eviction While L.A. Tries to Buy
     Their Property," *Capital and Main*, January 25, 2023, https://capitaland-
     main.com/hillside-villa-tenants-face-eviction-while-l-a-tries-to-buy-
     their-property.

36. Phoenix Tso, "Will the City Help Chinatown Tenants? Emails Show
     Officials Dragging Their Feet," *LA Public Press*, January 27, 2024, https://
     lapublicpress.org/2024/01/will-the-city-help-chinatown-tenants-emails-
     show-officials-dragging-their-feet/.

37. Knock LA Editorial, "Dear Mitch, Don't Evict Us," *Knock LA*, January 23,
     2020, https://knock-la.com/dear-mitch-dont-evict-us-8ed407d86f70/.

38. Tracy Rosenthal, "Inside LA's Homeless Industrial Complex," *New Repub-
     lic*, May 19, 2022, https://newrepublic.com/article/166383/los-ange-
     les-echo-park-homeless-industrial-complex.

39. Margot Kushel, MD, and Tiana Moore, PhD, *Toward a New Understanding:
     The California Statewide Study of People Experiencing Homelessness* (UCSF
     Benioff Homelessness and Housing Initiative, June 2023), https://homeless-
     ness.ucsf.edu/sites/default/files/2023-06/CASPEH_Report_62023.pdf.

40. Los Angeles Homeless Services Authority, "LAHSA Releases Results of

2023 Greater Los Angeles Homeless Count," June 29, 2023, https://www.lahsa.org/news?article=927-lahsa-releases-results-of-2023-greater-los-angeles-homeless-count; Kirsten Moore Sheeley et al., *The Making of a Crisis: A History of Homelessness in Los Angeles* (UCLA Luskin Center for History and Policy, January 2021), https://luskincenter.history.ucla.edu/wp-content/uploads/sites/66/2021/01/LCHP-The-Making-of-A-Crisis-Report.pdf.

41. Gale Holland and Christine Zhang, "Huge Increase in Arrests of Homeless in L.A. — but Mostly for Minor Offenses," *Los Angeles Times*, February 4, 2018, https://www.latimes.com/local/politics/la-me-homeless-arrests-20180204-story.html; Matt Tinoco, "One in Three Times the LAPD Used Force in 2018 It Involved a Homeless Person," *LAist*, March 12, 2019, https://laist.com/news/lapd-homeless-report-force-citation.

42. Ananya Roy et al., *(Dis)Placement: The Fight for Housing and Community after Echo Park Lake* (Los Angeles: UCLA Luskin Institute on Inequality and Democracy, 2022), https://escholarship.org/uc/item/70r0p7q4, 73.

43. Ayman Ahmed, interview with Tracy Rosenthal, Los Angeles, February 2022.

44. Emily Alpert Reyes, "Homeless People and Activists Protest at Echo Park Lake, Call for Meeting with Councilman," *Los Angeles Times*, January 24, 2020, https://www.latimes.com/california/story/2020-01-24/homeless-activists-protest-echo-park-lake.

45. Knock LA Editorial, "Dear Mitch, Don't Evict Us," *Knock LA*, January 23, 2020, https://knock-la.com/dear-mitch-dont-evict-us-8ed407d86f70/.

46. "Homelessness Audit: Interim Housing and Shelter Bed Data" (LA City Controller, December 5, 2023), https://controller.lacity.gov/landings/interim-housing-audit.

47. Rosenthal, "Inside LA's Homeless Industrial Complex."

48. CDC, "Responding to Coronavirus Disease 2019 (COVID-19) among People Experiencing Unsheltered Homelessness: Interim Guidance," Centers for Disease Control and Prevention, March 22, 2020, https://web.archive.org/web/20200401162155/https://www.cdc.gov/coronavirus/2019-ncov/need-extra-precautions/unsheltered-homelessness.html?CDC_AA_refVal=https%3A%2F%2Fwww.cdc.gov%2Fcoronavirus%2F2019-ncov%2Fcommunity%2Fhomeless-shelters%2Funsheltered-homelessness.html.

49. Liam Fitzpatrick, "The Echo Park Bathroom Saga: How the City Hates Homeless People," *Knock LA*, May 21, 2020, https://knock-la.com/echo-park-lake-bathrooms-closed-homelessness-los-angeles-cbf71222f14d/.

50. Ahmed, interview.

51. Larry Gordon, "Echo Park Lake Reopens after Two-Year Makeover," *Los Angeles Times*, June 15, 2013, https://www.latimes.com/local/la-xpm-2013-jun-15-la-me-0616-echopark-lake-20130616-story.html; Erika Aguilar, "MAP: Judge Allows Next Step in Proposed Echo Park Gang Injunction (Updated)," *LAist - KPCC*, August 22, 2013, https://www.kpcc.org/2013-08-21/court-hearing-on-city-of-los-angeles-proposed-echo.

52. Gale Holland, "A 5% Rent Increase Would Push 2,000 Angelenos into Homelessness, Study Warns," *Los Angeles Times*, August 2, 2017, https://www.latimes.com/local/lanow/la-me-ln-rent-increase-homelessness-20170802-story.html.

53. Jon Rodney, "Resilience in an Age of Inequality: Immigrant Contributions to California" (California Immigrant Policy Center, 2017), https://www.scribd.com/document/337336889/Resilience-In-An-Age-of-Inequality-Immigrant-Contributions-Report-2017-edition.

54. Brenda, interview by Tracy Rosenthal, Los Angeles, February 2022.

55. Benjamin Oreskes and Doug Smith, "How a Commune-like Encampment in Echo Park Became a Flashpoint in L.A.'s Homelessness Crisis," *Los Angeles Times*, March 13, 2021, https://www.latimes.com/homeless-housing/story/2021-03-13/echo-park-encampment-exposes-bigger-la-homeless-issues.

56. Benjamin Oreskes, "Echo Park Lake Reopens, with New Grass, New Paint and No Tents," *Los Angeles Times*, May 26, 2021, https://www.latimes.com/homeless-housing/story/2021-05-26/echo-park-repoens-and-fences-abound.

57. Roy et al., *(Dis)Placement*.

58. Erin McCormick, "'Homelessness Is Lethal': US Deaths among Those without Housing Are Surging," *The Guardian*, February 7, 2022, sec. US news, https://www.theguardian.com/us-news/2022/feb/07/homelessness-is-lethal-deaths-have-risen-dramatically.

59. Gustavo Otzoy, interview by Tracy Rosenthal, Los Angeles, February 2022.

60. Roy et al., *(Dis)Placement*, 67.

61. Roy et al., *(Dis)Placement*, 68.

62. Roy et al., *(Dis)Placement*, 92.

63. Ahmed, interview.

64. After Echo Park Lake Research Collective, "Blueprint For the Future: Unhoused Tenant Organizing in Los Angeles," *Radical Housing Journal* 4, no. 1 (July 11, 2022): 177–81.

65. Echo Park Rise Up, *A New Vision for Homelessness*, YouTube, October 14, 2020, https://www.youtube.com/watch?v=2rMAbS62xvw.

66. Andres de Ocampo, "Echo Park Lake Reopening Proves to Be Bittersweet," *Los Angeles Downtown News*, June 2, 2021, http://www.ladowntownnews. com/news/echo-park-lake-reopening-proves-to-be-bittersweet/article_ af884586-bffe-11eb-b766-2b7849e47ffb.html.

67. Leilani Farha (@leilanifarha), "I Am Watching with Alarm the Forced Eviction of #homeless People in LA's #EchoPark. EchoPark Is an Example of What Happens When Govts Don't Understand Homeless Encampments as Human Rights Claims and Homeless People as Human Rights Defenders. Https://T.Co/hfJmfFHMJC," X (formerly Twitter), March 27, 2021, https://twitter.com/leilanifarha/status/1375784081057837058.

68. LAHSA, "Project Roomkey Participant Agreement," Los Angeles Homeless Services Authority, September 2, 2021, https://www.lahsa.org/documents?id=4462-project-roomkey-participant-agreement.pdf.

69. Otzoy, interview.

70. End State Violence (@AlmostKelvin), "Please read and share this the statement written by the residents of Echo Park lake. It's truly remarkable." X (formerly Twitter), March 23, 2021, https://twitter.com/AlmostKelvin/status/1374450400967893002.

71. Isaac Scher, "Op-Ed: LAPD Violence in Echo Park Enforced Class Divisions, Not Public Safety," *Los Angeles Times*, April 3, 2021, https://www.latimes.com/opinion/story/2021-04-03/echo-park-lapd-violence-protests-eviction.

72. Ktown for All (@ktownforall), "@mitchofarrell Had a Fence Constructed around the Perimeter of Echo Park Lake Overnight and Has Turned the Lake into an Open Air Prison. Many Unhoused Residents Were Blindsided When They Woke up to a Fence Enclosing Them in. Those on the Outside Are Trying to Get through to Bring in Food and Resources. Screenshots of Reporting This Morning by Emily Alpert Reyes (LA Times) and Libby Denkmann (KPCC) #echoparkriseup," Instagram, March 25, 2021, https://www.instagram.com/p/CM2iFMvANcW/.

73. Kevin Rector and Emily Alpert Reyes, "LAPD to Review Echo Park Homeless Encampment Response," *Los Angeles Times*, April 6, 2021, https://www.latimes.com/california/story/2021-04-06/lapd-to-review-echo-park-homeless-encampment-response.

74. "Echo Park Rehabilitation: After Action Report," Los Angeles Police

Department, 2021, https://www.lapdpolicecom.lacity.org/080321/BPC_21-145.pdf, 30.

75. "Echo Park Rehabilitation," 8.

76. Otzoy, interview.

77. Otzoy, interview.

78. Beyond the European projects of mass social housing construction, we shift our horizons to Latin America, where the struggle of the poor has long been merged with the struggle to redistribute land. Brazil's Landless Workers' Movement (MST), with an informal membership of almost two million people, uses collective occupation to redistribute land to landless people. Groups of fifty to five hundred people organize to occupy unused, under-used, or misused land, building their own housing and farming organic produce for local and international sale. MST's reclamations often target land stolen through colonization, forced evacuation, or military occupation; enforce broken treaties or unfulfilled promises to redress specific Indigenous claims; and protect land from environmental degradation, deforestation, and oil extraction. This strategy has secured land—both housing and the means to make a living on it—for hundreds of thousands of Brazil's poor. Of course, unlike in the United States, the social function of land is enshrined in Brazil's constitution. MST can appeal to that constitution for both political legitimacy and material protection. Indigenous reclamation is emboldened by histories of socialist redistribution, and vice versa. Still, MST relies on extralegal action too: long-term occupations, backed up by large-scale eviction blockades.

79. Garcia, interview.

80. Garcia, interview.

81. Anne Orchier, interview by Tracy Rosenthal and Leonardo Vilchis, Los Angeles, June 2022.

82. Garcia, interview.

83. Garcia, interview.

www.ingramcontent.com/pod-product-compliance
Lightning Source LLC
Jackson TN
JSHW011948131224
75386JS00042B/1622

ABOUT THE AUTHORS

Tracy Rosenthal is a cofounder of the LA Tenants Union whose writing on housing and homelessness has been published in the *New Republic, The Nation*, the *LA Times*, and elsewhere. Rosenthal is now on rent strike in New York City.

Leonardo Vilchis has been organizing tenants in Boyle Heights for more than thirty years. Trained in liberation theology, Vilchis cofounded Union de Vecinos in 1996 to stop the demolition of the Pico Aliso public housing projects, winning the right of return for two hundred and fifty families. In 2015, he cofounded the LA Tenants Union to organize tenant power across Los Angeles. Vilchis was activist-in-residence at the UCLA Luskin Institute on Inequality and Democracy in 2020 and now serves on the advisory board of its Housing the Third Reconstruction research project.

INDEX